d to

JOHN BULL'S
Letter to Lord Byron

JOHN BULL'S
Letter to Lord Byron

EDITED BY

ALAN LANG STROUT

NORMAN

UNIVERSITY OF OKLAHOMA PRESS

1947

By Alan Lang Strout

The Life and Letters of James Hogg, I (1770–1825)

Lubbock, Texas, 1946

John Bull's Letter to Lord Byron

Norman, 1947

Publishing Division of the University

Composed and printed at Norman, Oklahoma, U.S.A.

by the University of Oklahoma Press

First Edition

Editor.—Why, we live in an age that will be much discussed when 'tis over—a very stirring, productive, active age—a generation of commentators will probably succeed—and I, for one, look to furnish them with some tough work.

Noctes Ambrosianae of March, 1822

PREFACE

APPARENTLY within three months after his friend Christie's fatal duel with John Scott of the *London Magazine*—a duel occasioned by his squibberies in *Blackwood's Magazine* between 1817 and 1821—John Gibson Lockhart, under the signature "John Bull," published a critical pamphlet on Byron's *Letter to W. L. Bowles* and the first two cantos of *Don Juan;* and then spent an agonizing three weeks in May and June, 1821, wondering whether his father-in-law Walter Scott, and the world in general, would discover the authorship of his latest pseudonymous sin and masterpiece. In 1941, through the kindness of the authorities of the William L. Clements Library of the University of Michigan, I first began transcribing Lockhart's letter to Croker there; but the first microfilm contained Lockhart's side of the correspondence alone; and it was only later when I received from the library a few miscellaneous letters, including several from Croker to Lockhart, that I was able to fit the two halves of the crossword puzzle together and definitely establish the authorship of Lockhart's *Letter to Byron on Don Juan* edited here.

The *Letter* should add to Lockhart's reputation as a critic, but I am not sure that it will add to his reputation as a man, particularly among those who, even today, persist in regarding him as a critical "Scorpion." After studying Lockhart for a good many years now, I admire him more and more warmly. The only error I personally have ever had to forgive him is his softening the vicious passage on Leigh Hunt in his first article on the "Cockney School" in *Blackwood's Magazine* of October, 1817.[1] No doubt the youth of not quite twenty-three feared that Hunt might sue the magazine for libel, and perhaps William Blackwood insisted upon the change. But either Lockhart should never have written the article, or, if he was ashamed of it, he should have repudiated it entirely —not have changed it just enough to escape a lawsuit. The whole incident, if it illustrates Scottish caution, is a little too close to illustrating cowardice to suit me. Lockhart's other critical excesses I am ready to forgive, partly for his age, partly for his Age. To me, the *Letter to Lord Byron* contains nothing to be ashamed of, though the reference, say, to S. T. Coleridge and J. T. Coleridge— "not the madman, but the madman's idiot nephew"—is a trifle strong (and all the stronger lifted from the context) even for 1821.

The *Letter to the Right Hon. Lord Byron by John Bull,* 1821, used in this study comes from a photostat ob-

[1] Hall Caine, I think, first pointed out the difference between the original passage and the later passage when William Blackwood reissued the suppressed number of October, 1817: "His [Leigh Hunt's] poetry resembles that of a man who has kept company with kept-mistresses. His muse talks indelicately like a tea-sipping milliner girl."

After an insinuation to the effect that perhaps Leigh Hunt is an unfortunate woman disguised in yellow breeches, the first edition contains the following paragraph, which was struck out in all subsequent editions:

"Some excuse for him there might have been, had he been hurried away by imagination or passion. But with him Indecency is a Disease, and he speaks unclean things from perfect inanition. The very Concubine of so impure a wretch as Leigh Hunt would be to be pitied, but alas for the Wife of such a Husband! For him there is no charm in simple Seduction; and he gloats over it only when accompanied with Adultery and Incest."—Sir T. Hall Caine, *Cobwebs of Criticism* (London, Stock, 1883), 141.

tained from the New York Public Library. I must thank that library; and, in addition, express my appreciation to the Clements Library of the University of Michigan, the Morgan Library of New York, and the National Library of Scotland for permission to print unpublished letters in their possession. As for individuals, Professor S. C. Chew has heartened me by assuring me that the *Letter* is worth republishing. Professor R. M. Wardle has helped me with Appendix A and Professors L. C. Stevens and A. B. Strehli with Appendix B. Professor W. B. Gates and I supervised Mrs. Christine Warren Stewart's thesis when she edited Lockhart's *Letter* at Texas Technological College. To "G. G. L." my thanks are due, since he was kind enough, in *Notes and Queries,* to spot two quotations unknown to me, leaving unidentified only two lines, "Turn cold regards upon the reverend man" and "Know when you are well," which Lockhart quotes in the original. I have been guilty of the grossest self-plagiarism in quoting from published articles of earlier years in the discussion of John Wilson and Lockhart. I have a dreadful feeling that the first sentence in the third paragraph of section two of the Introduction may come from some well-known history of the Napoleonic era: I quote it from an unpublished paper read some years ago before the "Questers" in Lubbock, Texas.

Appendix A, "Byron in Blackwood's Magazine," has nothing directly to do with the *Letter* proper; but to the bibliographer and the specialist, it will, I hope, prove useful. Any correction will gratify me as much as the corrector.

ALAN LANG STROUT

Lubbock, Texas
June 23, 1947

CONTENTS

ILLUSTRATIONS

JOHN BULL'S
Letter to Lord Byron

JOHN G. LOCKHART

From a sketch by Daniel Maclise
in *Fraser's Magazine,* August, 1830

INTRODUCTION

1. A Bibliographical Baker's Dozen

THE PRINCIPAL OBJECT of the present publication is to give the world an easily accessible copy of John Gibson Lockhart's *Letter to Byron on Don Juan*. Yet something of the background must be given, and for the general reader interested in that background, a bibliography may better come at the beginning than at the end of this volume.

Walter Graham's book, *English Literary Periodicals* (New York, Nelson, 1930), surveys the whole subject of periodical literature in Great Britain; Arthur R. D. Elliot's chapter "Reviews and Magazines in the Early Years of the Nineteenth Century" in the twelfth volume of *The Cambridge History of English Literature* (Cambridge, Eng., Cambridge University Press, 1916) gives an admirable discussion of the chief serial publications from the *Edinburgh Review* to *Fraser's Magazine;* and Professor Harold A. Innis's recent article, "The English Press in the Nineteenth Century: An Economic Approach," in the *University of Toronto Quarterly,* October, 1945, offers an admirable general survey, in less than twenty pages, of English newspapers and magazines of the last century. William Bates's *The Maclise Portrait-Gallery* (London, Chatto and Windus, 1873) includes thumbnail sketches along with excellent portraits of many leading periodical writers. For the *Edinburgh Review,* Henry Lord Cockburn's *Memorials of His Time* (London, Appleton, 1856) is as good a book as any by a contemporary, and Professor D. Nichol Smith's introduction to *Jeffrey's Literary Criticism* (London, H. Frowde, 1910) is as good a book as any by a later writer. For the *Quarterly Review,* one may read that good old stand-by, Samuel Smiles's *A Publisher and His Friends: Memoirs and Correspondence of John Murray* (London, John Murray, 1891, 2 vols.); just as for *Blackwood's Magazine,* one may read Mrs. Margaret Oliphant's *Annals of a Publishing House: William Blackwood and His Sons* (Edinburgh and London, William Blackwood, 1897). Dr. Miriam M. H. Thrall has more recently discussed *Fraser's Magazine* in *Rebellious Fraser's* (New York, Columbia University Press, 1934). Very different from such sympathetic or, at any rate, objective productions as those thus far listed are Hall Caine's *Cobwebs of Criticism* (London, Stock, 1883) and Albert Mordell's *Notorious Literary Attacks* (New York, Boni and Liveright, 1926), which emphasize the scurrilous and objectionable in the periodical criticism of a century ago. Specialized scholarly studies range from the identification of articles as in Professor Myron F. Brightfield's "Lockhart's *Quarterly* Contributors" in *Publications of the Modern Language Association (PMLA),* June, 1944, to the effects such articles had on particular victims as in Professor Harold E. Briggs's "Keats's Conscious and Unconscious Reactions to Criticisms of *Endymion*" in the same series of volumes, December, 1945.

The standard work dealing with Byron's relation to contemporary reviews and, indeed, with Byron's treatment by contemporaries generally remains Professor Samuel C. Chew's *Byron in England* (London, John Murray,

1924). A recent doctoral thesis, Dr. Paul G. Trueblood's *Flowering of Byron's Genius* (Palo Alto, Stanford University Press, 1945), discusses Byron in the reviews more particularly; just as another recent doctoral thesis, Dr. Elizabeth F. Boyd's *Byron's "Don Juan": A Critical Study* (New Brunswick, N. J., Rutgers University Press, 1945), discusses the sources of *Don Juan.*

2. *Concerning Three Great Periodicals*

Since Lockhart's *Letter to Byron on Don Juan* is a sort of expanded magazine article—the sort of article that, considerably telescoped, he might have contributed to *Blackwood's Magazine*—a brief survey of the background of periodical literature of the age may now be presented. After generalizing on the whole subject, I shall consider the *Edinburgh Review,* begun in 1802; the *Quarterly Review,* begun in 1809; and *Blackwood's Magazine,* begun in 1817. I shall pass over the *Quarterly* very briefly: first because space is limited; secondly, because the *Quarterly* is simply the antithesis of the *Edinburgh;* and thirdly, because what is said of *Blackwood's Magazine* parallels generally what might be said of the *Quarterly.*

Johnson once told Boswell that an imprudent publication, in early life, by one of his friends, would not do the man much harm—"it may, perhaps, be mentioned in an election." In the first third of the nineteenth century it was certain to be mentioned in a magazine. "In reviewing," exclaims the editor in the first of the *Noctes Ambrosianae, Blackwood's Magazine,* XI, March, 1822, "in reviewing, in particular, what can be done without personality? Nothing, nothing. What are books that don't express the personal characters of their authors; and who can review books, without reviewing those who wrote them?"

With the violent championing of, or the fierce resistance to, the repressive measures of government during the Napoleonic wars and, after 1815, with the "strong sensations" left in the wake of war, one can understand how impossible it is to overestimate the importance of politics in periodical criticism of the early nineteenth century. To their opponents a Whig or liberal in that age resembled, I suppose, a Communist in our own day; and to their opponents a Tory or conservative resembled (I do not mean to be too cutting) a Southern Democrat of today. Naturally Tories and Whigs did not love one another. Any reader of Hazlitt knows how political blindness affected constantly one of the clearest visions in English literature, how, for example, he could write the last paragraph on Scott in the *Spirit of the Age* (1825): Is not Scott one, he asks,

> who joined a gang of desperadoes to spread calumny, contempt, infamy, wherever they were merited by honesty or talent on a different side . . .—who being (by common consent), the finest, the most humane and accomplished writer of his age, associated himself with and encouraged the lowest panders of a venal press . . . , showing no remorse, no relenting or compassion towards the victims of this nefarious and organized system of party-proscription, carried on under the mask of literary criticism and fair discussion, insulting the misfortunes of some, and trampling on the early graves of others.

"I should be willing to kneel to him," Hazlitt remarked in a conversation with Jeffrey, who had offered to introduce him to Sir Walter, "but I could not take him by the hand."

Fierceness and personality, then, were the accepted and legitimate privileges of the periodical criticism of 150 years ago. They gave to reviews "some dash and brilliancy," undeniably lost in a softer age when "the laws of combat place buttons on the foils."

The power of the review rested upon the fact that not only its readers but its contributors as well were united. Of obvious importance to periodical criticism is the fact of anonymity. While anonymity had the important advantage of fusing the personality of the contributor in the personality of the magazine, of giving a coalescent effect to the whole publication, it had the obvious disadvantage of giving an opportunity to print the personally vindictive without a chance of being discovered. With the thoughtless, youthful, and robust contributors to *Blackwood's Magazine,* this was, in the early years of that publication, a temptation to which they often yielded. In her *Annals of a Publishing House,* Mrs. Oliphant gives an amusing picture, as late as 1842, of the grievous funk of Samuel Warren when the brothers Blackwood considered signing his name to a review of Dickens he had written.

Whatever his qualifications as a critic, Francis Jeffrey of the *Edinburgh Review* shines by comparison with his contemporaries. There is always a tendency to confuse the obvious distinction between inability to judge, as posterity will judge, contemporary poetry, and brutal attacks for political reasons upon the author of contemporary poems. At a time when Tory publications like the *Quarterly Review* and *Blackwood's Magazine* were absolutely flaying "Cockney" victims looked upon as revolutionary or "infidel," the editor of the *Edinburgh* criticized without political venom, and showed, moreover, an overscrupulous desire to let his victims know his authorship, rather than shield himself by anonymity. He sent his article on *Madoc* to Southey when that poet paid a visit to Edinburgh, so that he could meet his reviewer or not, as he chose;[1] he sent a manly letter to Scott with the number of the *Edinburgh* that contained the critique on *Marmion*;[2] he wrote Mrs. Grant of Laggan in September, 1811:

> When I review the works of my friends, if I can depend on their magnanimity as much as I think I can on yours, I let them know what I say of them before they are led out to execution. When I take up my reviewing pen I consider myself as entering the temple of truth, and bound to say what I think.[3]

In these days of the radio, the great newspaper, the magazine with a circulation in the hundreds of thousands or millions, it is difficult to realize the comparative calm

[1] Henry Lord Cockburn, *Life of Lord Jeffrey* (Edinburgh and London, William Blackwood, 1852, 2 vols.), I, 169.

When James Hogg teased Jeffrey to allow him to review Southey's *Roderick* in the *Edinburgh,* the editor wrote the Shepherd: "For Southey I have, as well as you, great respect, and when he will let me, great admiration; but he is a most provoking fellow, and at least as conceited as his neighbor Wordsworth. I cannot just trust you with his Roderick; but I shall be extremely happy to talk over that and other kindred subjects with you; for I am every way disposed to give Southey a lavish allowance of praise, and few things would give me greater pleasure than to find he has afforded me a fair opportunity. But I must do my duty according to my own apprehensions of it."—*The Poetical Works of R. Southey, Collected by Himself* (London, Longman, Brown, Green, and Longmans, 1844, 10 vols.), IX, *xviii;* hereafter referred to as Southey, *Poetical Works.* For Southey's letter to Hogg concerning *Roderick,* December 24, 1814, see Appendix C.

[2] J. G. Lockhart, *Memoir of the Life of Sir Walter Scott* (Edinburgh, Cadell; London, Murray and Whitaker, 1837, 7 vols.), II, 281.

[3] *Memoir and Correspondence of Mrs. Grant of Laggan,* ed. by J. P. Grant (London, Longman, Brown, Green, and Longmans, 1844, 3 vols.), I, 291.

of a century and a half ago. "I look upon the invention of reviews to be the worst injury which literature has received since its revival," Robert Southey grumbled to a friend in a letter of 1804.

> People formerly took up a book to learn from it, and with a feeling of respectful thankfulness to the man who had spent years in acquiring that knowledge, which he communicates to them in a few hours; now they look only for faults. Every body is a critic, that is, every reader imagines himself superior to the author, and reads his book that he may censure it, not that he may improve by it.[4]

And fifteen years later Keats wrote his brother George: "I have no doubt of success in a course of years if I persevere—but it must be [with] patience—for the Reviews have enervated and made indolent men's minds—few think for themselves." Nor are these remarks of Southey and Keats unnecessarily sour; for a leading authority on the period writes that "after 1794 superficial reading displaced heavy reading and the age of romantics began."[5] Perhaps the two poets were fortunate in living when they did: the tabloid, the pulp magazine, the comic section make even romantic superficiality seem fairly heavy by comparison with 1947.

With the whole weight of the magazine behind the anonymous reviewer, incalculable weight was given the articles in a review, even when a reader must have recognized the virulence of personality based on political antipathy. At the publication of Keats's *Lamia* in 1820, his publisher Taylor insisted that it was the attack of the

[4] C. C. Southey, *Life and Correspondence of Robert Southey* (London, Longman, Brown, Green, and Longmans, 1850, 6 vols.), II, 276–77.

[5] Harold A. Innis, "The English Publishing Trade in the Eighteenth Century," *The Manitoba Arts Review,* Winter, 1945, 23.

Quarterly Review in 1817, "imputing to Keats a certain political bias," that most stood in the way of his successful recognition as a poet," "at the thought of which the fiery publisher bursts out, 'Damn them (I say) who could act in so cruel a way to a young man of undoubted Genius.' "[6] *Blackwood's Magazine* with its "literary rowdyism" was even more blackguardly than the *Quarterly*. And if the "Cockney School" suffered from the Tory magazines, the "Lake School" in turn suffered from the Whig *Edinburgh*. In March, 1804, Southey informed his friend Rickman,

> Turner wrote me and complained heavily of Scotch criticism, which he seems to feel too much; such things only provoke me to interject Fool! and Booby! seasoned with the participle damnatory; but as for being vexed at a review—I should as soon be fevered by a flea-bite!

But the souring of Wordsworth, his and Southey's curious eagerness to let ages not their own decide their fame, depended undoubtedly, to large degree, on the adverse criticism of the periodicals. "Drafts upon posterity will not pass for current expenses," Southey wrote Reginald Heber in November, 1807, a pathetic reference surely, both as regards his finances then and his fame now. Wordsworth's confidence in posterity has something of pathos also. "My ears are stone-dead to this idle buzz," he wrote Lady Beaumont in May, 1807, concerning the critiques on *Poems in Two Volumes,* "and my flesh as insensible as iron to these petty stings." But he is less philosophical in a letter to Wrangham a couple of months later, when he

[6] Amy Lowell, *John Keats* (Boston and New York, Houghton Mifflin, 1925, 2 vols.), II, 449. (Keats's letter to his brother George, quoted above, comes from the same source, II, 185.)

pours out his wrath upon the critic "Legrice." And in his later years he grew, as was natural, sulky.

> There does not appear to be much genuine relish for poetical Literature in Cumberland [he wrote Moxon in 1833]; if I may judge from the fact of not a copy of my Poems having been sold there by one of the leading Booksellers, though Cumberland is my native Country.—Byron and Scott are I am persuaded the only *popular* Writers in that line, perhaps the word ought to be that they are *fashionable* Writers.[7]

If the reviews and public neglect affected the strong thus, sensitive poets like Keats, and Tennyson after him, suffered more deeply. Poetasters were crushed; of course, posterity does not care for that.

Yet it would be unfair to leave an impression that periodical criticism was altogether negative and "below the belt." Though that curiously "tiebeamless" person John Wilson praised Wordsworth in one number of *Blackwood's Magazine* only to attack him in the next, the warm approval of Wordsworth in "Maga" (as William Blackwood affectionately called his magazine) probably started—certainly extended—the poet's vogue after 1817. It is so easy today to quote startling passages of disapproval in early magazines, indeed, that I wish some aspirant for the doctor's degree would write a thesis considering only the complimentary reviews of contemporary poets in, say, the *Edinburgh* and the *Quarterly* reviews and in *Blackwood's* and *Fraser's* magazines. Just what poets, big and little, received praise, I wonder, and what was the proportion of

[7] Southey's letter of 1804 has already been quoted (see n. 4 above). The quotations from Wordsworth's letters may be found in Ernest de Selincourt's *The Letters of William and Dorothy Wordsworth: The Middle Years* (Oxford, The Clarendon Press, 1937, 2 vols.), I, 130–31, 134; and *The Later Years* (1939, 3 vols.), II, 664.

praise to blame? All doctoral theses must, it seems, be dull, but I should think this one less likely to be dull than most.

One minor matter may be considered in conclusion, the fact that periodical criticism sometimes affected the phrasing in later editions of a poem. In a famous review of Tennyson in the *Quarterly* of April, 1833, for example, John Wilson Croker refers to *A Dream of Fair Women,*

> in which the heroines of all ages . . . pass before his view. We have not time to notice them all, but the second, whom we take to be Iphigenia, touches the heart with a stroke of nature more powerful than even the veil the Grecian painter threw over the head of her father.
>
> ———"dimly I could descry
> The stern blackbearded kings with wolfish eyes,
> Watching to see me die.
>
> The tall masts quivered as they lay afloat;
> The temples, and the people, and the shore;
> One drew a sharp knife through my tender throat—
> Slowly,—and *nothing more!*"
>
> What touching simplicity—what pathetic resignation—he cut my throat—"*nothing more!*" One might indeed ask, "what *more*" she would have?

Tennyson changed the last stanza to:

> The high masts flickered as they lay afloat;
> The crowds, the temples, wavered, and the shore;
> The bright death quivered at the victim's throat—
> Touched—and I knew no more.

Similarly in a review of *Crabbe's Poems, Edinburgh Review,* April, 1808, Jeffrey refers to Wordsworth's poem *Matthew*. The poet, he says, represents this gray-haired rustic pedagogue as a sort of half crazy, sentimental person, overrun with fine feelings, constitutional merriment, and a most humorous melancholy. Here are the two stanzas in which this consistent and intelligible character is portrayed. The diction is at least as new as the conception.

"The sighs which Mathew heard [heav'd] were sighs
    Of one tired out with *fear and madness;*
The tears which came to Mathew's eyes
    Were tears of light—*the oil of gladness.*

Yet sometimes, when the secret cup
    Of still and serious thought went round,
He seemed as if he *drank it up,*
    He felt with spirit so profound.

Thou *soul,* of God's best *earthly mould,*" &c.

Wordsworth disregarded the last italicizations, but he did change the first stanza to:

The sighs which Matthew heaved were sighs
    Of one tired out with fun and madness;
The tears that came to Matthew's eyes
    Were tears of light, the dew of gladness.

Perhaps the poet would have made the change himself later, independently. But in these days of the automobile and the airplane, a tear is certainly better described as "the dew of gladness" than "the oil of gladness."

A. *The Edinburgh Review,* 1802

After eight months of brilliant ridicule against the Whigs, the witty *Anti-Jacobin* had ceased, its object accomplished, in 1798. At least one important effect resulted from its critiques: "The later strictures against the lake school," writes Professor Haller, "and the anathemas heaped upon Southey by Byron, Hazlitt, and others for turncoating were all in part the result of the satire of The Anti-Jacobin."[8] Other periodicals, before the *Edinburgh Review,* as Walter Scott wrote George Ellis in 1808, "had become extremely mawkish."[9] With articles subscribed gratuitously, with policy in complete control of cautious publishers, no wonder. And then, one stormy evening in March, 1802, at Jeffrey's "elevated mansion" in Buccleuch Place, quite casually Sydney Smith suggested setting up a Whig review. Henry Lord Brougham in his account of the event first quotes Sydney Smith, then adds his own recollections. According to Smith, towards the end of his residence in Edinburgh he and Brougham happened to be present at Jeffrey's residence:

> I proposed that we should set up a review: this was acceded to with acclamation. I was appointed editor, and remained long enough in Edinburgh to edit the first number. The motto I proposed was, *"Tenui musam meditamur avena"*—We cultivate literature on a little oatmeal. This was too near the truth to be admitted, and so we took our grave motto from Publius Syrus, of whom none of us had ever read a line. When I left Edinburgh, the Review fell into the stronger hands of Jeffrey and Brougham, and reached the highest point of popularity and success.

Brougham in his account insists that Smith was never editor: "He read over the articles, and so far may be said to have edited the first number; but regularly constituted editor he never was." Brougham continues:

8 William Haller, *The Early Life of Robert Southey* (New York, Columbia University Press, 1917), 232.

9 Lockhart, *Scott,* II, 214.

I think we owed the motto for the Review to the painstaking and solemn Horner, who, being as incapable of understanding a joke as Smith was of writing the "Principia," discovered in Publius Syrus, a comic writer of the time of Caesar, the motto which we adopted, and which Horner thought better than Smith's "oatmeal" suggestion.[10]

Brougham thinks, and Henry Lord Cockburn in his *Life of Jeffrey* thinks also, that Smith had previously broached the subject of a review to Horner and Jeffrey; but Brougham adds that he himself first heard of the plan at Jeffrey's dinner table on this stormy night of March, 1802, and that at this time it was first seriously discussed. Not only did Smith suggest the review; according to Brougham, it was his overpowering vivacity that evening that overcame the timorousness of Jeffrey; and, according to the same author, it was also Smith who, in his brief supervision of the first number, advised Archibald Constable, the publisher of the *Edinburgh,* to pay a permanent salary to his editor as well as to remunerate handsomely *every* contributor.

"Jeffrey's inconceivable timidity" prevented publication until October; Brougham writes that "he kept prophesying failure in the most disheartening way." But the success of the first number "was far beyond any of our expectations"; as Lord Cockburn says, "The effect was electrical."[11] After the first number Jeffrey assumed the editorship, a position which he held until 1829, with an independent salary: at first three hundred pounds, later five hundred pounds. For the first three numbers, contribu-

[10] *The Life and Times of Henry Lord Brougham Written by Himself* (Edinburgh and London, Blackwood, 2nd ed., 1871, 3 vols.), I, 246–48. Other references from Brougham are taken from I, 251, 252, 254.

[11] *Life of Lord Jeffrey,* I, 131.

tors sent in their articles gratuitously; thereafter they received a minimum rate of ten guineas a sheet (i.e., sixteen pages[12]). "The scale of payment is a *minimum* of sixteen guineas a sheet," Jeffrey wrote James Mill in January, 1811, "though two-thirds of the articles are paid much higher—averaging, I should think, from twenty to twenty-five guineas a sheet on the whole number."[13] This increased rate of payment shows how amazingly the new work prospered. "Baron von Lauerwinkel" (Lockhart), one of the cruelest critics of the Whigs, in his first article in *Blackwood's Magazine,* (II, March, 1818, 674), wrote of the *Edinburgh* and Jeffrey:

> "The journal, conducted by this gentleman in a provincial town of Britain, has, notwithstanding it is opposed by the whole weight of ministerial influence, a circulation far beyond any periodical work in England"—upwards of 15,000.

The ingenuous enthusiasm of the statement brought a footnote of protest to the sentence in *Blackwood's Magazine* itself. Actually, the maximum circulation of both

12 See Walter Scott's letter to his brother Tom, November 19, 1809, in *The Letters of Sir W. Scott,* ed. by H. J. C. Grierson and others (London, Constable, 1932, 12 vols.), II, 131.

13 Alexander Bain, *James Mill. A Biography* (London, Longmans, Green, 1882), 112. The quotation is changed slightly to fit my text.

14 "In 1829 . . . on an average, every London newspaper was read by thirty people."

"For a short time after November, 1816, the sale of Cobbett's twopenny *Political Register* rose to 40,000 or 50,000 a week: a figure many times larger than that of any other newspaper; and, too, a single copy frequently served for scores of auditors."—A. Aspinall, "Circulation of Newspapers in the Early Nineteenth Century," *The Review of English Studies,* XXII, January, 1946, 30, 39–40.

For reviews and magazines, moreover, bound volumes might be edited later. Thus, besides the four quarterly numbers of the *Edinburgh* and the *Quarterly* reviews, bound volumes, containing two numbers each, might run through a large number of editions; see *Cambridge History of English Literature,* XII, 158.

Edinburgh and *Quarterly* reviews in 1818 and 1819 was about 14,000, and this never was exceeded. If, however, a dozen or two dozen persons read each issue, the circulation was a considerable one.[14]

Jeffrey was, of course, a conservative neither in politics nor (according to his contemporaries) in religion. His father, "a careful and discerning parent," felt such anxiety to shield his offspring from the intellectual taint of Whiggism that he forbade him to attend Miller's lectures at Glasgow and, later, Stewart's lectures at the University of Edinburgh.[15] The parent's efforts availed nothing. Jeffrey could not forget the persecution of the victims in the sedition trials of 1794, the year he was admitted to the bar, and he turned Whig though he knew that he was shutting himself off from preferment, utterly. He was not alone. Archibald Alison, a Tory and a contributor to *Blackwood's Magazine,* admits grudgingly that almost all men of spirit joined the Whigs at the Scotch bar,[16] and George Gleig, also a contributor to *Blackwood's,* quotes, ironically to be sure, Henry Cockburn's self-complacent statement that in 1817 "the Tories being unable to find among themselves any one qualified to sit upon the bench were forced against their will to make the Whig Gillies a judge."[17]

Though he scathingly attacked the erotic poems of "Thomas Little" in the *Edinburgh* and had as a result to

15 Walter Bagehot, "The First Edinburgh Reviewers," in *Literary Studies* (London, Longmans, Green, 1884, 2 vols.), I, 24.

16 *Autobiography of Archibald Alison,* ed. by Lady Alison (Edinburgh and London, Blackwood, 1883, 2 vols.), I, 128.

17 *Quarterly Review,* January, 1864, 116, 453. Just the opposite was true when the Whig reformers were in power: see Charles Dickens's account of the public dinner given in his honor at Edinburgh in 1841 in John Forster, *Life of C. Dickens* (Philadelphia, J. B. Lippincott, 1872, 3 vols.), I, 259. In Edinburgh, political clanship lingered long!

fight his famous "leadless duel" with Tom Moore in 1806, though he approved such a work as Bowdler's *Family Shakespeare* in a review of October, 1821, and though a modern scholar speaks of his "essentially ethical outlook on literature,"[18] Jeffrey's flippancy, conversational levity, and intellectual inquisitiveness probably account for his being considered a sort of skeptical ogre by his contemporaries. Thus in a letter to John Murray of June 18, 1809, Gifford speaks of the "flippant impiety" of the *Edinburgh Review,*[19] and so late as 1897 Andrew Lang in his *Life and Letters of Lockhart* (London, John C. Nimmo, 1897, 2 vols.), I, 173ff., devotes eight pages to sustaining Lockhart's attack upon the religion (what Lang calls "that chilly ignorant skepticism") of the periodical. Certainly in politics and in social questions Jeffrey was a reformer: "The people are both stronger, and wiser, and more discontented, than those who are not the people will believe," he wrote Horner, October 26, 1809.[20] But he was a moderate reformer only and had small sympathy with more radical Whigs, or "Jacobins." John Thelwall's poems he had reviewed with what he thought just ridicule in April, 1803. In December of that year Thelwall came to Edinburgh and tried to give a course of public lectures on elocution and oratory. He published at the time a violent pamphlet against Jeffrey for having "confederated" against him and taken a principal part in spoiling his first appearance in the lecturing hall. Jeffrey published a pamphlet in reply. From the critic's article on "Cobbett's Political Register," July, 1807, again we find

18 Merritt Y. Hughes, "The Humanism of Francis Jeffrey," *Modern Language Review,* XVI, 247.

19 Smiles, *A Publisher and His Friends,* I, 158.

20 Cockburn, *Life of Lord Jeffrey,* I, 197.

FRANCIS JEFFREY

From *Kay's Edinburgh Portraits* (1816)

JOHN WILSON CROKER

From a sketch by Daniel Maclise
in *Fraser's Magazine,* September, 1831

that Jeffrey had small sympathy for another famous Whig contemporary:

> Instead of the champion of establishment, of loyalty, and eternal war with all revolutionary agency, he has become the patron of reform and reformers; talks hopefully of revolutions; scoffingly of Parliament; and cavalierly of the Sovereign.—X, 387.

That the "infidel" *Edinburgh Review,* frankly advocating peace with France, and constantly with its verve, independence, and Olympian finality irritating the Tories, was not suppressed, is surprising. Yet Walter Scott frequently contributed to the magazine in its early years; his pride in the publication as an outgrowth of Scottish literature apparently overcame temporarily his Tory prejudice.

Since Jeffrey gave the tone of his personality to his periodical in the two hundred contributions he published there, a word may be said of his character. When Mrs. John Wilson first came to Edinburgh in 1811 or 1812, she described Jeffrey in a letter to her sister as "a horrid little man, held in as high estimation here as the Bible." Twenty years later Richard Sheil wrote Lady Morgan from Edinburgh, July, 1821:

> I met Jeffery [*sic*] and Macaulay here at dinner; Jeffery has the most astounding volubility I ever witnessed. . . . I witnessed at Sir J. Mackintosh's his introduction to Wordsworth, for the *first* time. The latter grinned horribly, a ghastly smile.[21]

And in another letter to Southey (who considered Jeffrey

[21] *Lady Morgan's Memoirs,* ed. by W. H. Dixon (London, W. H. Allen, 1862, 2 vols.), II, 324.

an "animalcule") Henry Taylor thus acutely characterizes the editor of the *Edinburgh* in November, 1835:

> There came from him, with a sort of dribbling fluency, the very mincemeat of small talk, with just such a seasoning of cleverness as might serve to give it an air of pretension. Nevertheless, I believe the little man has his merits; I believe him to be good-natured, and, in his shallow way, kind-hearted.[22]

From his reviews it is easy to gather the general characteristics of Jeffrey: (1) a strong partiality for the Scotch; (2) a distinct demand for morality; (3) a flippant irony or cocksureness; (4) a cautious and frequently confusing method of mixing praise and blame; (5) a distrust for the new and "romantic," and a partiality for the orthodox in poetry.

In the first number of the *Edinburgh* (October, 1802), Jeffrey opens his critique on Southey's *Thalaba* with this dictum:

> Poetry has this much, at least, in common with religion, that its standards were fixed long ago, by certain inspired writers, whose authority it is no longer lawful to call in question; and that many profess to be entirely devoted to it, who have no *good works* to produce in support of their pretensions.

The bumptious self-confidence of youth is here apparent. The wretched pun detracts irritatingly from the seriousness of the pronouncement. The review of Thomas Campbell's *Gertrude of Wyoming,* half a dozen years later, in April, 1809, gives a norm of what the critic demands in poetry. This work has neither "the babyism or the anti-

[22] *Correspondence of Henry Taylor,* ed. by Edward Dowden (London, Longmans, Green, 1888), 68.

quarianism" of contemporary poetry; "we rejoice once more to see a polished and pathetic poem, in the old style of English pathos and poetry."

It appears to us, therefore, that by far the most powerful and enchanting poetry is that which depends for its effect upon the just representation of common feelings and common situations, and not on the strangeness of its incidents, or the novelty or exotic splendor of its scenes and characters.

(This last pronouncement seems like a perfect summary of the best in Wordsworth's poetry; yet the compliment is paid to Campbell!) Twenty years later in his last literary review, that of Felicia Hemans's *Poems* (October, 1829), the critic retrospectively remarks that of all the poets of his age, Rogers and Campbell "have the longest withstood the rapid withering of the laurel." During his editorship of the *Edinburgh* Jeffrey seems haunted by the bogy-dread that Scott—or Wordsworth—may be ready to introduce "a new school" of poetry.

An authority in our own day, Professor D. Nichol Smith, says on the last page of his introduction to *Jeffrey's Literary Criticism* that "the opinions expressed in the early numbers of the *Edinburgh Review* have permeated English criticism to an extent not commonly recognized." I have not attempted to consider the range, variety, and importance of Jeffrey's criticism but have tried only to give some idea of the casual, almost accidental, inception of the *Edinburgh Review* and some idea of the general critical characteristics of its editor. Now, in conclusion, I shall discuss briefly Jeffrey's comments on the "Lake School" and on Byron.

The articles on Coleridge—and I consider the review of *Christabel* in September, 1816, one of the stupidest ever written—are largely the work of William Hazlitt and may be found in the tenth volume of Waller and Glover's *The Collected Works of William Hazlitt,* (London, J. M. Dent, 1902–1904, 12 vols.). Jeffrey may have added editorial touches, and of course his was the responsibility for allowing the pieces to appear in the *Edinburgh Review.* As for Wordsworth, anyone reading that work for the first time will be astonished at the frequency with which the critic brings out his praise for a poet under discussion by contrasting him with Wordsworth or, more surprising still, with Wordsworth and Southey. (Occasionally, to be sure, he holds Wordsworth up to lesser poets as an example of what they might accomplish.) Perhaps Jeffrey's general attitude towards the Lake poet best appears in his review of John Wilson's *City of the Plague* in December, 1816, for here, in considering the disciple, he takes a whack at the master. The critic mentions three abominations that he cannot stand:

(1) Conceit and self-admiration, when united with only ordinary talent
(2) Perversity or affectation
  (a) A silly ambition at singularity
  (b) An unfortunate attempt to combine qualities which are truly irreconcilable
  (c) An absurd predilection for some fantastic style or manner
(3) Moral defect, i.e., traces of petty jealousy and envy of rival genius

In reviews dealing with Wordsworth directly, the first and most important is the discussion of Wordsworth's *Poems* in October, 1807. The reviewer early refers to the *Lyrical Ballads.* This volume, in spite of its "occasional vulgarity, affectation, and silliness," deserves praise, he says, for its "strong spirit of originality, of pathos, and natural feeling." Later he writes of the poems of 1807 that their author "always writes good verses, when, by any accident, he is led to abandon his system."—XI, 228.

> Even in the worst of these productions, there are, no doubt, occasional little traits of delicate feeling and original fancy; but these are quite lost and obscured in the mass of childishness and insipidity with which they are incorporated.—XI, 231.

In short Wordsworth, led astray by his theory, in his second publication "appears like a bad imitator of the worst of his former productions." The "Ode on the Intimations of Immortality" the critic considers "the most illegible and unintelligible part of the publication."—XI, 227.

The notorious opening sentence "This will never do," in Jeffrey's article of November, 1814, on *The Excursion* has, we think, been somewhat overquoted; for in general his review of the piece is a good one, and, with splendid oases to be sure, the poem has been well described by a critic in our own day, as one of the Saharas of verse. Certainly he is "a little quietly facetious" in his review of "The White Doe of Rylestone," in October, 1815—which he considers "the very worst poem we ever saw imprinted in a quarto volume" (XXV, 355)—when he makes the observation that its author has "dashed his Hippocrene with too large an infusion of lake water" (p. 356). Finally, in a discussion of *Memorials of a Tour on the Continent,* November, 1822, the editor of the *Edinburgh Review* remarks: "The Lake School of Poetry, we think, is now pretty nearly extinct" (XXXVII, 449), and speaks of the "sort of emphatic inanity" (p. 450) to which Wordsworth has sunk.

Though of the *Lucy Poems* Jeffrey quotes only the two feeblest lines of one:

> "O mercy! to myself I cried,
> If Lucy should be dead!"[23]

though he returns with irritating frequency to mention of *The Thorn,* I have personally always had a sneaking sympathy for the critic, for Wordsworth is the most uneven of poets and surely disapprobation of a writer for the absurdities in his worst productions easily leads to critical misunderstanding of the beauties in his best. If Mr. Edgar Guest were to publish a second *Hamlet* tomorrow, I doubt if I should recognize its greatness. Certainly from his articles generally, one realizes that Francis Jeffrey had enthusiasm for external nature. Apparently he had made up his mind about Wordsworth and the *Lyrical Ballads* and let his initial prejudice color his later attitude. It seems to me that Jeffrey in his reprinted *Essays* of 1844 somewhat unnecessarily apologizes, in his treatment of Wordsworth, for "an asperity which should be reserved for objects of moral reprobation."

Though he showed an irritating habit of coupling Coleridge and Wordsworth with the Laureate, Jeffrey did succeed in placing Southey for posterity. One may not agree when the critic objects to an ambition of "an undisciplined and revolutionary character" as poet, in the author of *Madoc* (1805); one may possibly not acquiesce in his antipathy to the oriental scenery and "the eternal enchantment" of the poet's works; but one is hardly likely to dispute his opinion of the writer's *Roderick*—which Jeffrey considered Southey's most powerful production:

23 In the review of Crabbe's *Poems, Edinburgh Review,* XII, 136.

"The author is a poet undoubtedly; but not of the highest order."—*Edinburgh Review,* XXV, 1.

Jeffrey on Byron is an interesting study. A moral Scotsman, the critic could appreciate the poet only in part; yet when he is not disturbed by Byron's unorthodoxy and what he terms his "mysticism," he consistently finds praise. Just as he commends in his article on the first two cantos of *Childe Harold* (February, 1812), the excellent descriptions, in spite of the lack of any central unity in the poem, so he commends the "tone of self-willed independence and originality of the whole composition" (XIX, 467), even though he considers the hero of the piece, unfortunately, "Satanic." Just as he extols *The Giaour* (July, 1813), and *The Corsair* and *The Bride of Abydos* (April, 1814), for their unparalleled rapidity of narrative, their life, verve, and activity, so he does not altogether admire the style and diction, and expresses the fear that Byron's gloomy heroes show a tendency to pervert our moral nature: "There is no intellectual dignity or accomplishment about any of his characters; and no very enlightened or equitable principles of morality."—XXIII, 228. Just as he shows discrimination enough in his review of the third canto of *Childe Harold* (December, 1816), to see in the poem a Wordsworthian (and Southeyan!) influence (XXVII, 278); and just as he states that Byron—as far at least as depth of impression on his readers is concerned—surpasses all contemporary poets (p. 277), so he still sees in the hero of the poem "a sort of demoniacal sublimity" (p. 279); and quotes some of the finest stanzas to illustrate his own impenetrability to the beautiful when he explains what "the sometimes abundantly mystical" means to him. Thus he quotes a stanza and a half, including

Ye stars! which are the poetry of heaven!

with the comment, "These are mystical enough, we think; but what follows is nearly as unintelligible as some of the sublimities of Wordsworth himself" (p. 304). Whereupon he quotes a stanza from the description of the thunderstorm in the Alps:

> Could I embody and unbosom now
> That which is most within me . . . .

In August, 1817, he is puzzled by that "extraordinary performance" *Manfred,* which he considers "very strange and "not very pleasing" (XXVIII, 418): "There are great faults, it must be admitted, in this poem;—but it is undoubtedly a work of genius and originality" (p. 429); in February, 1818, he applauds the attractive caustic lightness of *Beppo,* pointing out that in one stanza, at least, the unknown author "seems to have caught a spark from the ardent genius of Byron" and remarking that there are "traits of Lord Byron" elsewhere in the poem (XXIX, 306, 307); in July, 1821, he regards *Marino Faliero* "as a failure, both as a Poem and a Play," for it is "generally very verbose, and sometimes exceedingly dull" (XXXV, 271, 284). In his last important review, "Lord Byron's Tragedies" of February, 1822 (for in his remarks on *Heaven and Earth* a year later he discusses also Moore's *Loves of the Angels), Cain* and *Don Juan* are too much for him. He does not critically eviscerate *Don Juan,* though he does blow the poem up a bit: Byron "has no priestlike cant or priestlike reviling to apprehend from us" (XXXVI, 447); instead he compares the poet, to his disadvantage, with Walter Scott. The latest authority on Byronic criticism considers Jeffrey's comments on *Don*

Juan in this review both tolerant and just. Here, he says, we have "true *literary* criticism for the first time."[24]

B. *The Quarterly Review,* 1809

The *Quarterly Review* had a much less spectacular and spontaneous inception than the *Edinburgh Review,* which it was founded to combat: it was middle-aged from the beginning. In fact, it was the Tory periodical, just as the *Edinburgh Review* was the Whig. Did space permit, it would be pleasant to outline this periodical's treatment of Byron or to consider Croker's famous flaying of Keats, but merely to give a taste of Gifford's publication—which he edited, except for a few months, until Lockhart became editor at the end of 1825—I shall here outline briefly the attacks on Shelley and on Hazlitt.

The subject of Shelley's treatment by the *Quarterly* was considered by Walter Graham in an article "Shelley's Debt to Leigh Hunt and the Examiner," in *PMLA* some twenty years ago (XL, 185 ff.). In Croker's review of Leigh Hunt's *Foliage* (January, 1818), as Graham points out, Shelley's expulsion from Oxford, his abandonment of his wife, and his atheism are spoken of, though Shelley is not mentioned by name (*Quarterly Review,* XVIII, 328–29). In J. T. Coleridge's violent review of *The Revolt of Islam* (April, 1819), the first version, *Laon and Cythna,* is reviewed also, for the sake of emphasizing the matter of incest in the poem. The work, though the critic admits beautiful passages, is "unsupportably dull, and laboriously obscure" (XXI, 463). Shelley is accused of the endeavor "to pull down our churches, level our Establishment, and burn our bibles" (p. 468), as he would do away with mar-

24 Trueblood, *Flowering of Byron's Genius,* 46.

riage and repeal the laws against incest. This young man belongs to a "miserable crew of atheists or pantheists" (p. 461). Finally, in October, 1821, occurs an equally fierce attack, by William Sydney Walker, on *Prometheus Unbound*. The poem, says the critic, is "absolutely unintelligible," a dictum admirably proved by the review that follows. The literary absurdities are enumerated—"to his long list of demerits he has added the most flagrant offences against morality and religion" (XXVI, 177); fortunately for humanity, the poet has taken the precaution "to temper irreligion and sedition with nonsense" (p. 178).[25]

William Hazlitt naturally receives, likewise, in the *Quarterly* unmitigated abuse compounded of bitterness and condescension. In the first review devoted to his work, that on his *Round Table* (April, 1817), he is called "a sour Jacobin"; the author feels it unnecessary to answer his "loathsome trash." In January, 1818, was published Hazlitt's *Characteristics of Shakespeare's Plays,* the whole edition of which, with the prompt insertion of Jeffrey's complimentary notice in the *Edinburgh Review,* "went off in six weeks; and yet it was a half-guinea book." Then

25 Professor Graham failed to note, and I do not know whether anybody else has since noted, that after Lockhart became editor of the *Quarterly,* he treated Shelley kindly in a couple of incidental references. Thus in his review of the *Translations of Goethe's "Faust"* (June, 1826), he goes out of his way to speak kindly of Shelley's translations in general, especially of certain Greek translations in his *Posthumous Poems.* "One department of literature," he writes, "has, without doubt, sustained a heavy loss in the early death of this unfortunate and misguided gentleman" (XXXIV, 148). Once more, in Lockhart's virulent attack on Hunt, Keats, and Hazlitt in the review of Leigh Hunt's *Lord Byron and Some of His Contemporaries* (March, 1828), reference is made to "the unfortunate Mr. Shelley" (XXXVII, 425). To be sure, the *Quarterly* justifies the separation of Shelley from his children in a long excerpt in an article entitled "Equitable Jurisdiction," in January, 1829 (XXXIX, 193ff.).

appeared a violently hostile criticism in the *Quarterly Review,* annihilating, with irony and insolent personality, "the blundering ignorance" and "senseless and wicked sophistry of this writer."

> I had [writes Hazlitt] just prepared a second edition—such was called for—but then the *Quarterly* told the public that I was a fool and a dunce; and more, that I was an evil-disposed person; and the public, supposing Gifford to know best, confessed it had been a great ass to be pleased where it ought not to be, and the sale stopped completely.[26]

The critic of Hazlitt's *Lectures on the English Poets* (July, 1818) considered most of the lectures "completely unintelligible"; the reviewer of the *Political Essays* (July, 1819) was horrified at "this angry buffoon" and "this slanderer of the human race"; finally, the author of the last attack on Hazlitt in the *Quarterly,* in a review of *Table Talk* (October, 1821), devotes his pages to proving Hazlitt a "Slang-whanger." Meanwhile the victim had relieved his feelings (and the feelings of at least one reader of the twentieth century) with his *Letter to William Gifford* (1819) and, though it was not printed until more than one hundred years after his death when it was edited by Charles Whibley, his fiery *Reply to Z,* who had called him "pimpled Hazlitt" in *Blackwood's Magazine.*

c. *Blackwood's Magazine,* 1817

Instead of appearing only four times a year like the *Edinburgh* and the *Quarterly, Blackwood's Magazine* appeared monthly, and was warmer, sprightlier, and saucier than the grave quarterlies. Humorous personalities lighten its pages—the coinages "Cockney School" originated

[26] W. Carew Hazlitt, *Memoirs of William Hazlitt* (London, Richard Bentley, 1867, 2 vols.), I, 228, 229.

by Lockhart, and "pimpled Hazlitt" probably originated by Wilson; the references to "Sir Egerton Breeches" (XI, 291), and Hazlitt's "Stable-Talk" (X, 556); the flippant "A Few Words to Our Contributors" in the early volumes, as, for example, "A. S. should put another S. to his name. He amply deserves it"; the shortest review in the magazines, that on *The Craniad, or Spurzheim Illustrated* (June, 1817):

> The Craniad is the worst poem we have now in Scotland. The author has it in his power at once to decide the great craniological controversy: Let him submit his skull to general inspection, and if it exhibits a single intellectual organ, Spurzheim's theory is overthrown.—I, 288.

Incidentally, *The Craniad* was published by "Blackwood, Edinburgh, 1817." It may be pointed out that Blackwood had a share in Leigh Hunt's *Story of Rimini,* venomously and persistently attacked in the magazine also. Indeed, no more glaring example of partisan bile appears than in the Tory reviews of Hunt's poem. John Wilson Croker in the *Quarterly* of January, 1816, objects throughout his article to the poetic principles of the author, ridiculing his grammar, phraseology, versification, and narrative technique: the story "he has, at least, the merit of telling . . . with decency." John Gibson Lockhart in *Blackwood's Magazine* of October, 1817, on the other hand, considers the poem itself "not undeserving of praise." He concentrates his attack upon the irreligious and unpatriotic character of Hunt, and upon the immorality of the theme of the poem.

Something will be said of Lockhart in the next section; here we may notice another Scotchman, John Wilson, who profoundly influenced his friend and colleague in these early years; for Wilson acted with Lockhart as lieutenant of William Blackwood, when that redoubtable publisher after ridding himself of his early editors Cleghorn and Pringle—who had slopped along with a very humdrum periodical from April to October, 1817—sent a bombshell into Edinburgh and the world in general with the first number of a very different publication in October, 1817.

A dozen years before this event, in October, 1805, in his twentieth year, John Wilson, gentleman commoner at Magdalen College, Oxford, purchased some ground on Lake Windermere. Here it was that, after his brilliant graduation in March, 1807, the winner of the first Newdigate Prize in poetry settled in his cottage of Elleray. Through diffidence he had been unwilling to intrude upon Wordsworth during his early visits to the Lake District; but by 1808 he had made the acquaintance of the poet and his family, and until early in 1815, when he left the Lake District for Edinburgh, he lived on intimate terms with them, as the letters of Dorothy Wordsworth show. His high spirits, personal magnetism, social charm, and unconventionality had given him "a most heterogeneous reputation" at the university, where all sorts of legends gathered about his name. "Wilson of Mallens," indeed, was famous not merely for his intellect, but also for his pugilistic ability, his leaping, and his cockfighting. At Wastdale Head, on one occasion, the young man's sense of humor so overpowered him that he deceived Wordsworth and the others by pretending to be drowning, diving under water whenever the English poet attempted to rescue him.[27] Similarly at the Horse-head [Wytheburn]

[27] James Payn, *The Lakes in Sunshine* (London, Simpkin, 1870), 89.

Christopher North [Wilson's later pen name in *Blackwood's Magazine*] made horseplay on a certain occasion when, as Hartley Coleridge tells us, Wilson of Elleray had come to the public-house with his sporting friends. They were just sitting down to table when he took his neighbor's gun and fired up the chimney, with the result that all leapt to their feet, and when the smother had cleared away the whole room was black with soot; but Christopher North was so merry over this practical joke that the company were obliged perforce to forgive him.[28]

Compared with Wilson, Wordsworth cut no figure. "Nay, nay, he [Wordsworth] was over feckless i' his hands. I never seed him at feasts, or wrestling, he hadn't owt of Christopher Wilson in him . . . ," a disgusted builder of the Lake District told H. D. Rawnsley in 1870.[29] After his marriage in May, 1811, to Jane Penny, "the leading belle of the Lake country," Wilson divided his time between Elleray and, in winter, the Scottish bar in Edinburgh; and upon the loss of his fortune he took up his residence at his mother's house in Edinburgh in the spring of 1815. Two years later he became a leading spirit, along with Lockhart, in *Blackwood's Magazine,* which, as has been noted already, in the number of October, 1817, almost blew up publisher, contributors, and magazine itself with a number that contained James Hogg's "Chaldee Manuscript," Wilson's famous attack on Cole-

28 H. D. Rawnsley, *Past and Present at the English Lakes* (Glasgow, J. MacLehose and Sons, 1916), 218.

29 *Wordsworthiana,* ed. by William Angus Knight (London and New York, Macmillan, 1889), 99. Another native told Rawnsley likewise, contrasting Wordsworth and Wilson: "Wudsworth was never no cock-fighter nor wrestler, no gaming man at all, and not a hunter, and as for fishing he hedn't a bit o' fish in him, hedn't Wudsworth—not a bit of fish in him."—*Ibid.,* 114.

ridge's *Biographia Literaria,* and Lockhart's equally famous first assault upon Leigh Hunt and the "Cockney School."

Since Wilson so deeply influenced Lockhart in the early years of their association with *Maga,* something more needs be said of one of the most breath-taking of reviewers, from whose critiques one can today find alternately praise or blame of many of his chief contemporaries. Sentimental or macabre poet, brilliant talker of "Modern Athens," lecturer in moral philosophy for thirty years at the University of Edinburgh, as well as contributor of thousands of pages to *Blackwood's Magazine,* John Wilson, enemy of Whigs, flayer of "Cockneys," was the personal friend of De Quincey, Wordsworth, Lockhart, Walter Scott, Thomas Campbell, and James Hogg. Alexander Smith in *A Summer in Skye* (1865) writes:

> It may be said that Burns, Scott, and Carlyle are the only men really great in literature,—taking *great* in a European sense—who, during the last eighty years, have been connected with Edinburgh. I do not include Wilson in the list; for although he was splendid as any of these for the moment, he was evanescent as a Northern light. In the whole man there was something spectacular.

Wilson's genius, as Andrew Lang well says, "was perhaps the most unbalanced in the history of literature."[30] And Thomas Carlyle in his *Journal* of April, 1854, records the death of Wilson and reflects how this man and he "lived apart, as in different centuries."

> Wilson [he writes] seemed to me always by far the most *gifted* of all our literary men, either then or still; and yet in-

[30] *Life of Lockhart,* I, 125.

trinsically he has written nothing that can endure. The central gift was wanting.

Now a man who, if not "great," has the fortune to be spectacular has a certain importance to his age. As rhapsodist, as inspired improviser, "Christopher North" at least delighted his generation with the Brobdingnagian humor of the *Noctes Ambrosianae,* most popular of serials before *Pickwick Papers.* All too often, indeed, "North" appears to have been content merely to turn on the spigot of his emotions in order to produce a leading article. Nothing is easier, in considering Wilson, than to allow his obvious lapses into the sentimental to make us forget that this first-honors man of Oxford had the clearest perception of what the public wanted; that from his desire to be immediately popular he was quite willing (scorning posterity) to use the most immediate appeal to his age; that after the loss of his fortune in 1815 he supported himself almost entirely through articles in *Blackwood's Magazine* and through lectures that, however lacking in philosophical profundity, made him the most popular as well as the most stimulating teacher in the University of Edinburgh. Despite his sentimental rhapsodizing at his worst and, it must be added, his diffuseness, Wilson has, moreover, certain merits: gaiety at his best, and geniality, and gusto; amazing versatility that justifies a quantitative rather than a qualitative consideration of his achievement; brilliance as an occasional critic, greater brilliance as a large-brush describer of Scottish scenery and the landscapes of Windermere; greatest brilliance as a masculine humorist (best shown in the *Noctes Ambrosianae*); and a big bow-wow style that appealed particularly to contemporary youth—witness Branwell Brontë, Frank Carr

JOHN WILSON

Reproduced from a copyrighted photograph by permission of Francis Caird Inglis, Edinburgh

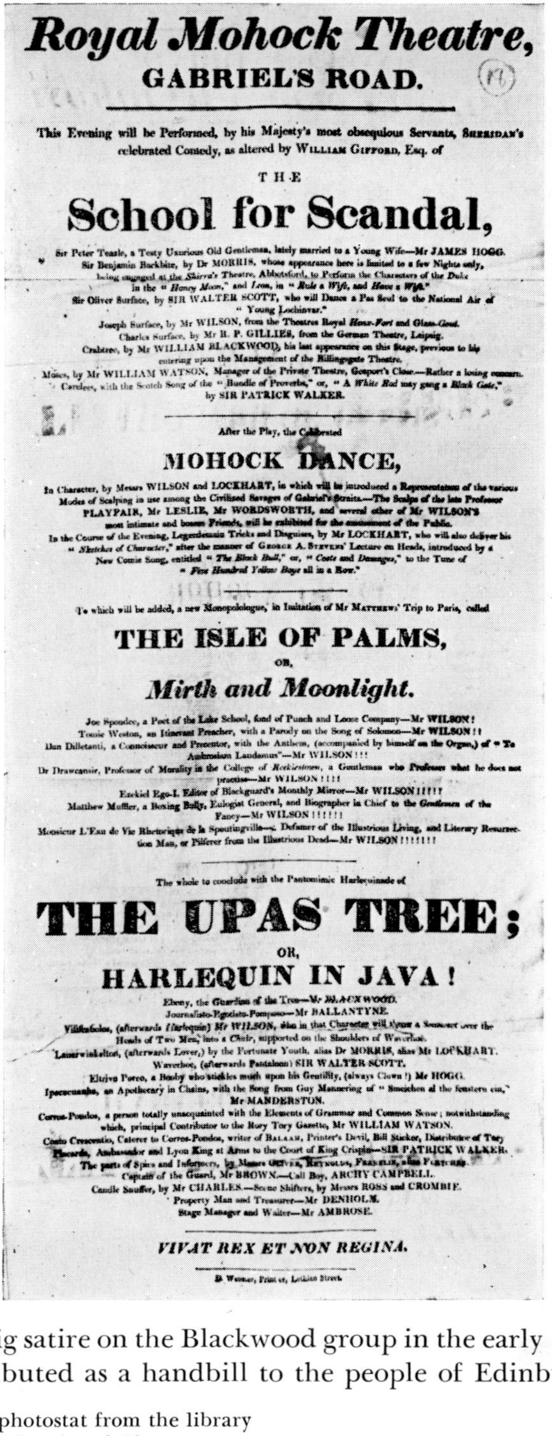

Royal Mohock Theatre,

GABRIEL'S ROAD.

This Evening will be Performed, by his Majesty's most obsequious Servants, SHERIDAN'S celebrated Comedy, as altered by WILLIAM GIFFORD, Esq. of

THE

School for Scandal,

Sir Peter Teazle, a Testy Uxorious Old Gentleman, lately married to a Young Wife—Mr JAMES HOGG.
Sir Benjamin Backbite, by Dr MORRIS, whose appearance here is limited to a few Nights only, being engaged at the *Shirra's* Theatre, Abbotsford, to Perform the Characters of the *Duke* in the "*Honey Moon*," and *Leon*, in "*Rule a Wife, and Have a Wife.*"
Sir Oliver Surface, by SIR WALTER SCOTT, who will Dance a Pas Seul to the National Air of "Young Lochinvar."
Joseph Surface, by Mr WILSON, from the Theatres Royal *Hour-Fort* and *Glass-Gout*.
Charles Surface, by Mr R. P. GILLIES, from the German Theatre, Leipsig.
Crabtree, by Mr WILLIAM BLACKWOOD, his last appearance on this Stage, previous to his entering upon the Management of the Billingsgate Theatre.
Moses, by Mr WILLIAM WATSON, Manager of the Private Theatre, Gosport's Close.—Rather a losing concern.
Careless, with the Scotch Song of the "Bundle of Proverbs," or, "A *White Rod* may gang a *Black Gate*," by SIR PATRICK WALKER.

After the Play, the Celebrated

MOHOCK DANCE,

In Character, by Messrs WILSON and LOCKHART, in which will be introduced a Representation of the various Modes of Scalping in use among the Civilized Savages of Gabriel's Straits.—The Scalps of the late Professor PLAYFAIR, Mr LESLIE, Mr WORDSWORTH, and several other of Mr WILSON'S most intimate and bosom Friends, will be exhibited for the amusement of the Public.
In the Course of the Evening, Legerdemain Tricks and Disguises, by Mr LOCKHART, who will also deliver his "*Sketches of Character*," after the manner of GEORGE A. STEVENS' Lecture on Heads, introduced by a New Comic Song, entitled "*The Black Bull*," or, "*Costs and Damages*," to the Tune of "*Five Hundred Yellow Boys* all in a Row."

To which will be added, a new Monopolologue, in Imitation of Mr MATTHEWS' Trip to Paris, called

THE ISLE OF PALMS,

OR,

Mirth and Moonlight.

Joe Spondee, a Poet of the Lake School, fond of Punch and Loose Company—Mr WILSON!
Tomie Weston, an Itinerant Preacher, with a Parody on the Song of Solomon—Mr WILSON!!
Dan Dilletanti, a Connoisseur and Precentor, with the Anthem, (accompanied by himself on the Organ,) of "Te Ambrosium Laudamus"—Mr WILSON!!!
Dr Drawcansir, Professor of Morality in the College of *Reekiestown*, a Gentleman who Professes what he does not practise—Mr WILSON!!!!
Ezekiel Ego-I. Editor of Blackguard's Monthly Mirror—Mr WILSON!!!!!
Matthew Muffler, a Boxing Bully, Eulogist General, and Biographer in Chief to the *Gentlemen* of the Fancy—Mr WILSON!!!!!!
Monsieur L'Eau de Vie Rhetorique de la Spoutingville—Defamer of the Illustrious Living, and Literary Resurrection Man, or Pilferer from the Illustrious Dead—Mr WILSON!!!!!!!

The whole to conclude with the Pantomimic Harlequinade of

THE UPAS TREE;

OR,

HARLEQUIN IN JAVA!

Ebony, the Guardian of the Tree—*Mr BLACKWOOD.*
Journalisto-Egotisto-Pomposo—Mr BALLANTYNE.
Villifacfulos, (afterwards *Harlequin*) *Mr WILSON*, who in that Character will throw a Somerset over the Heads of Two Men, into a *Chair*, supported on the Shoulders of Waverloo.
Lauerwinkelton, (afterwards Lover,) by the Fortunate Youth, alias Dr MORRIS, alias Mr LOCKHART.
Waverloo, (afterwards Pantaloon) SIR WALTER SCOTT.
Eltrivo Porco, a Booby who stickles much upon his Gentility, (always Clown!) Mr HOGG.
Ipecacuanha, an Apothecary in Chains, with the Song from Guy Mannering of "Smeichen al the fenstern ein," Mr MANDERSTON.
Corrus-Pondos, a person totally unacquainted with the Elements of Grammar and Common Sense; notwithstanding which, principal Contributor to the Rory Tory Gazette, Mr WILLIAM WATSON.
Conto Crescentio, Caterer to Corrus-Pondos, writer of BALAAM, Printer's Devil, Bill Sticker, Distributor of Tory Placards, Ambassador and Lyon King at Arms to the Court of King Crispin—SIR PATRICK WALKER.
The parts of Spies and Informers, by Messrs OLIVER, REYNOLDS, FRANKLIN, alias FORTUNE.
Captain of the Guard, Mr BROWN.—Call Boy, ARCHY CAMPBELL.
Candle Snuffer, by Mr CHARLES.—Scene Shifters, by Messrs ROSS and CROMBIE.
Property Man and Treasurer—Mr DENHOLM.
Stage Manager and Waiter—Mr AMBROSE.

VIVAT REX ET NON REGINA.

D. Wemer, Printer, Lothian Street.

A Whig satire on the Blackwood group in the early 1820's distributed as a handbill to the people of Edinburgh

From a photostat from the library of the University of Glasgow

("Lancelot Cross"), N. P. Willis, George Gilfillan, Samuel Warren, Charles Lever, and even John Ruskin—and that has kept its appeal for various admirers from his own to the present day.[31]

As critic, be it granted, moods of the moment, not critical principles, were his guide. We might expect Jeffrey of the *Edinburgh Review,* Delphic oracle of the Whigs or liberals as has been shown, to hold a somewhat radical and "romantic" view of literature; Wilson, the Tory or conservative, to hold a conventional and decorously classical view of literature. Just the reverse is true. Jeffrey has sanity and restraint: we know, generally speaking, what he will say of any given writer. Wilson has freshness and floridity: we never know what he will say of any given writer; moreover, we have a shrewd suspicion that he himself does not know until he starts writing his critique. Jeffrey, too, is consistent in his views, whereas we may be fairly certain that sooner or later Wilson will contradict what he says on one occasion by something violently opposed to it on another. Jeffrey may be the safer guide, yet to a contemporary reader Wilson probably had the greater appeal from his very spontaneity and unpredictability. John Wilson, in short, substituted for a technic a pyrotechnic, and, impelled by his moods, spiked the canons of criticism for the applause, at least, of contemporaries. Yet taking all his work together, it may be said that if the early nineteenth century turned to Scott in the novel and to Byron in poetry, it turned to "Christopher North" in magazine writing.

31 "As a stylist, he has never received due recognition," writes Malcolm Elwin in *Victorian Wallflowers* (London, Jonathan Cape, 1934), 74–75. "Lamb and Hazlitt [as periodical writers] have come into their own, and the time for Wilson's recognition is long overdue."

As for the articles in *Maga,* perhaps enough is said generally if it is pointed out that William Blackwood, according to the present writer's computation, paid at least 830 pounds, in addition to legal expenses, for libel in the first five years of his magazine's existence.

Even today one's blood may boil at the "Elegy on my Tom Cat" on the last page of the review of *Adonais* in *Blackwood's Magazine* of December, 1821. Yet rather than recall such indefensible examples of the scorbutic, it is better perhaps to remind the reader of lighter touches buried in the mass of abuse leveled against the "Cockneys" in *Maga.* Thus "On the Cockney School of Poetry" (V, April, 1819) ends with amusing parodies of Hunt's critical essays, and with the following admirable parody of his poetry:

Sonnet on Myself

I love to walk towards Hampstead saunteringly,
And climb thy grassy eminence, Primrose Hill!
And of the frolicksome breeze, swallow my fill,
And gaze all round and round me. Then I lie
Flatlily on the grass, ruralily,
And sicken to think of the smoke-mantled city,
But pluck a butter-cup, yellow and pretty,
And twirl it, as it were, Italianly.
And then I drink hot milk, fresh from the cow,
Not such as they sell about the town; and then
I gaze at the sky with high poetic feeling,
And liken it to a gorgeously spangled ceiling;
Then my all-compassing mind tells me—as now,
And as it usually does—that I am foremost of men!

There is an attractive schoolboy sauciness in such a parody, just as there is an exasperating schoolboy exaggeration of bitterness all too often devoted by *Maga* to its enemies. Indeed, schoolboys are exactly what Lockhart and Wilson remind us of in these early years—Wilson always remained one: he never quite managed to grow up. Only schoolboys could have had the wicked ingenuity to send Leigh Hunt, at the time of the first attack upon him in the magazine, a letter containing a pretended confession of authorship of this attack, purporting to be from John Dalyell, himself smarting from a libelous description contained in the "Chaldee Manuscript" in the same number. Only schoolboys, again, could have introduced into Lockhart's review of Henry Luttrell's *Advice to Julia* (August, 1820) a quotation from the poem which runs:

> Perchance, a truant from his desk,
> Some lover of the picturesque,
> Whose soul is far above his shop,
> Hints to his charmer where to stop;
> And the proud landscape, from the hill, eye
> Which crowns thy terrace—Piccadilly!
> *Perchance Leigh Hunt himself is near,*
> *Just waking from a reverier—*
> Whispering, "My dear, while others hurry,
> "Let us look over into Surrey...."—VII, 522.

For the couplet concerning Hunt, which I have italicized, does not occur in the original.

As will appear shortly, in the fourth section of this introduction, the wits of *Maga* even pretended that a noted Whig, Jeremy Bentham, was the author of Lockhart's *Letter to Byron on Don Juan!* A sufficient idea of the grave and the light in *Blackwood's Magazine* appears in the outline of articles dealing with Lord Byron in Appendix A.

3. Croker and Lockhart

As has just been shown, the pre-Victorian age was a brutal one, at least in snuffing out fiery souls with an article; and of the Tory reviewers John Gibson Lockhart shared with John Wilson Croker the greatest contemporary hatred. William Charles Macready in his *Diary* of June 23, 1834, refers to "that puppy Lockhart"; N. P. Willis in the year following calls him "this reptile of criticism"; and George Gilfillan in *The Scottish Review* twenty years later contends that Lockhart was *Blackwood's Magazine's*

> presiding spirit. He indited the most impudent of its hoaxes. He told the most flagrant of its falsehoods. He wrote the most unjust of its criticisms. He improvised the most absurd and riotous of its witticisms and political squibs. He reviewed favorably the worst of his own books. He was, in short, its Evil Genius, giving it much of its inspiration, and almost the whole of its infamy.

Small need, therefore, to quote the author of an article in the *Eclectic Review* of January, 1863, who calls Lockhart "a morbid, bilious, ill-conditioned, cantankerous thing, disagreeable in mind and in body." The strictures against Lockhart might be multiplied a dozenfold against Croker, the "Counsellor Con Crowley" of Lady Morgan's *Florence M'Carthy* (1816), the "Rigby" of *Coningsby* (1844), and the "Wenham Wagg" of *Vanity Fair* (1847–48). A single contemporary opinion sums up the general antipartisan attitude: Croker was

> a man who would go a hundred miles through sleet and snow, to search a Parish Register, for the sake of showing that a man was illegitimate, or a woman older than she said she was.

No defense of Croker is necessary after Professor Myron F. Brightfield's able *John Wilson Croker* of 1940 (Berkeley, University of California Press); but the untimely death of Dr. Alexander Mitchell in Edinburgh during the recent World War has halted what might well have been the definitive biography of Lockhart—and we must still rely mainly on Andrew Lang's two volumes published in 1897, though material has been since accumulated in the National Library of Scotland that entirely outmodes this work of half a century ago. Before considering the relations of Croker and Lockhart in 1819, 1820, and 1821, then, let me give a brief sketch of Scott's son-in-law.

On April 29, 1820, Lockhart married Sophia Scott and in July of that year Walter Scott wrote Morritt:

> Lockhart is very much what you will like when you come to know him—much genius and a distinguishd scholar very handsome in face and person and only wanting something of the usage de monde. I mean there is a little want of ease in his manners in society. He does not laugh as thou doest Anthony—this is however speaking critically for he is neither conceited nor negligent in his manner. His powers of personal satire are what I dread most on his own account—it is an odious accomplishment and most dangerous and I trust I have prevaild on him to turn his mind to something better.

Some half a dozen years later, on April 13, 1826, Scott wrote to Lady Louisa Stuart also:

> I am delighted that Lockhart passes current with you. He really is a fine fellow a scholar a man of taste and point devise the gentleman. I am sometimes angry with him for an exuberant love of fun in his light writings which he has caught I think from Wilson a man of greater genius than himself perhaps but who disputes with low adversaries which I think

a terrible error and indulges in a sort of humor which exceeds the bounds of playing at ladies and gentlemen a game to which I have been partial all my life.

Wilson himself in the twenty-ninth of the *Noctes Ambrosianae* (November, 1826), puts into the mouth of the Ettrick Shepherd this description of Lockhart:

> Was n'at me that first prophesied his great abeelities when he was only an Oxford Collegian, wi' a pale face and a black toozy head, but an ee like an eagle's, and a sort o' lauch about the screwed-up mouth o' him, that fules ca'd no canny, for they couldna thole the meanin' o't, and either sat dumbfoundered, or pretended to be engaged to sooper, and slunk out o' the room?

That the real James Hogg liked and admired Lockhart appears (to quote only one example) from the following letter Allan Cunningham sent the Shepherd on December 23, 1828:

> You may remember when you wrote to me of Mr. Lockhart's coming to the *Quarterly Review,* that you told me of the [goodness] of his heart, and desired me to take up no man's song against him, but know him and feel him for myself. . . . I have found Lockhart one of the best, the kindest, and most unaffected friends I ever met. Now, he is no sayer of sweet and sugary things, which the very vain gape for and swallow, his words are few and to the point, and I have found them dictated by kindness and good sense. I like him for this, and for his scorn of all that is mean and sordid.[32]

Other eulogistic examples might be given also: Thomas Carlyle, for instance, whose vignettes in vinegar of his

32 Mrs. Mary Garden, *Memorials of James Hogg* (Paisley and London, Alexander Gardner, 1887), 220.

contemporaries lend zest to Victorian reminiscence, never felt real friendship for John Wilson though he retained a warm admiration for Lockhart, who did not strike him "as one of these damned literary men."

That Lockhart was guilty of critical excess in his early years is true: indeed, the publication here of his *Letter to Byron on Don Juan* of 1821 is another example of his youthful devil-may-care attitude. (That Walter Scott will discover the authorship seems his chief dread, as will appear in his letters to Croker considered in the next section.) But the present writer is somewhat weary of having Lockhart constantly condemned as a deliberate critical assassin whereas his colleague John Wilson's vivisections of his enemies—or his friends—in his "casual, incidental way" are always forgiven as the emotional sheet lightnings of the moment. Moreover, Lockhart in his later years learned sobriety, whereas the "tiebeamless" "Christopher North" was guilty of violent fustigations after 1826. At times, to be sure, Wilson suffered intensely for his articles, but usually he and William Blackwood seem to have forgotten the attacks themselves, as well as the commotion which they caused, a month after they were written and the excitement had died down. Blackwood never apologized for his magazine in after life; Wilson never seemed seriously to feel that there was anything to apologize for, though he frequently enough in his later productions expresses regret, jocosely, for his roughness, past and present.

Lockhart alone felt sorrow—or at least ever voiced his repentance privately or publicly. As introduction to his chapter on Lockhart's connection with Blackwood, Andrew Lang quotes the following letter to Haydon, written July 11, 1838, explaining the early attacks on the "Cockneys":

In the first place, I was a raw boy, who had never had the least connection either with politics or controversies of any kind, when, arriving in Edinburgh in October, 1817, I found my friend John Wilson (ten years my senior) busied in helping Blackwood out of a scrape he had got into with some editors of his Magazine, and on Wilson's asking me to try my hand at some squibberies in his aid, I sat down to do so with as little malice as if the assigned subject had been the Court of Pekin. But the row in Edinburgh, the lordly Whigs having considered *persiflage* as their own fee-simple, was really so extravagant that when I think of it now, the whole story seems wildly incredible. Wilson and I were singled out to bear the whole burden of sin, though there were abundance of other criminals in the concern, and by-and-by, Wilson passing for being a very eccentric fellow, and I for a cool one, even he was allowed to get off comparatively scot-free, while I, by far the youngest and least experienced of the set, and who alone had no personal grudges against any of Blackwood's victims, remained under such an accumulation of wrath and contumely, as would have crushed me utterly, unless for the buoyancy of extreme youth. I now think with deep sadness of the pain my jibes and jokes inflicted on better men than myself, and I can say that I have omitted in my mature years no opportunity of trying to make reparation where *I* really had been the offender. But I was *not* the doer of half the deeds you seem to set to my account, nor can I, in the face of much evidence printed and unprinted, believe that, after all, our Ebony (as we used to call the man and his book) had half so much to answer for as the more regular artillery which the old *Quarterly* played incessantly, in these days, on the same parties. . . .

I believe the only individuals whom *Blackwood* ever really and essentially injured were myself and Wilson. Our feelings and happiness were disturbed and shattered in consequence of that connection. I was punished cruelly and irremediably in my worldly fortunes, for the outcry cut off all prospects of professional advancement from me.

In this letter Lockhart gives a fuller apology than that which, so early as 1819, he had given publicly, if anonymously, in *Peter's Letters to His Kinsfolk* (Edinburgh and London, William Blackwood, 1819, 3 vols.), II, 210ff. He here apologizes for various articles in the early numbers of *Maga,* though he still justifies the attacks on the "Cockneys." In general exculpation of *Blackwood's* early numbers, Peter points out: (1) the extreme youth and inexperience of its writers; (2) their literary acquaintance with critical excesses of an earlier period; (3) a lack of plan and firm guidance—as long as a few articles were sound, there was room for the unrestrained.

They approached the lists of literary warfare with the spirit at bottom of true knights; but they had come from the woods and the cloisters, and not from the cities and haunts of active men, and they had armed themselves, in addition to their weapons of the right temper, with many other weapons of offence, which, although sanctioned in former times by the practice of the heroes in whose repositories they had found them rusting, had now become utterly exploded. . . .

They stained, in plain language, the beginning of their career with the sins of many wanton and malicious personal satires. . . . They must take the consequences of their own audacious folly, in committing, or permitting, such gross outrages upon all good feeling.

And in the last volume we read (III, 137):

But Mr. L[ockhart] is a very young person, and I would hope may soon find that there are much better things in literature than satire, let it be as good-humored as you will. Indeed, his friend W[astle] tells me he already professes himself heartily sick of it, and has begun to write, of late, in a quite opposite key.

Why, under the influence of Walter Scott, particularly after Lockhart's quarrel with John Scott of the *London Magazine* and Christie's fatal duel with the latter in the early days of 1821, did not Lockhart sever his allegiance to *Blackwood's Magazine?* Andrew Lang analyzes his devotion to Blackwood, aside from his monetary return from his articles, "to love of mischief, of freedom to indulge caprice, to friendship for Wilson, and regard for Mr. Blackwood." Besides all this, the "Scorpion" was, like Scott, a Tory.

Lockhart's direct debt to William Blackwood was, indeed, great. The publisher had paid him £ 300, or more, to travel in Germany in the vacation of 1817, for a "work in translation, to be written later."

Though seldom communicative on such subjects, he more than once alluded to the circumstance in after-life, and always in the same terms. "It was a generous act on Ebony's part, and a bold one too."[33] Blackwood made a shrewd investment, and Lockhart was true to his friends. Again, the manner in which the publisher shielded Wilson and Lockhart time and time again and, in a crisis, bore himself the brunt of the attacks upon his magazine; this, even leaving out of consideration the appeal Blackwood's sturdy character and personal magnetism made to Lockhart, held Lockhart, as it would hold most men, true. But the fundamental reason for his loyalty to his publisher lies fully as much in Lockhart's youthful camaraderie with the wild fraternity of *Blackwood's Magazine*. Mrs. Oliphant's pictures of the group in her book, *Wil-*

[33] George Gleig, *Quarterly Review,* CXVI, October, 1864, 452.

liam Blackwood and His Sons, are pleasant decidedly. "Most strange creatures" like De Quincey, volcanic Berserkers like Wilson and Captain Tom Hamilton, pachydermatous rustic geniuses like James Hogg, princes of butts like James Scott the Odontist, and later, scholarly humorists like Dr. William Maginn, do not happen every day to a youth in his early twenties.

That Lockhart's connection with *Blackwood's Magazine* was unfortunate, there can be little doubt. Viewed in one light, John Wilson, who spent his powers on periodical literature, is a gigantic failure. Yet contemporary fame sufficed for him; he did what he could do, well. Mrs. Gordon writes in the life of her father: "Periodical literature, it seems to me, was precisely the thing for which he was suited by temperament, versatility, and power." Lockhart, with a more complex character, with the powers of genius, is almost a tragic figure. Andrew Lang has written so admirably of this subject that he may be quoted once more:

> There was more in him, more of genius and power, than ever found full and free expression; he never realized all his energies, and not to do so is not to be happy, even as far as happiness is meant for mortals. . . . For Lockhart leaves, on a mind long and clearly occupied with him, an impression of thwarted force, of a genius that never completely found its proper path.

Perhaps not *Blackwood's,* but magazine writing, stunted Lockhart, as it did William Maginn—stunted only, for genius must flower in spite of "the spirit of levity, and the 'Imp of the Perverse' " (Lang, I, 124). My own explanation of Lockhart's personalities, that, Lang admits, "if not without example, went beyond even the Tory standard of the time" (I, 132), is sufficiently simple. Lockhart, it seems to me, wrote some of the fiercest reviews of the age because of his genius. In the articles on the "Cockney School" we find negatively what in his masterpiece, the *Life of Scott,* we find positively: the same clearness, the same self-repression, the same quietness and simplicity and vigor, but the first scrofulous with second-hand hate against men whom he knew not, the second rainbowed with a great understanding and a great love. Not to appear too much a special advocate, I feel that literary historians have not realized sufficiently the importance of "mob psychology" in explaining the early lapses of *Maga.* Wilson, emotionally reckless, Lockhart, a youth in his early twenties, later Maginn, as emotionally reckless as Wilson, even more precocious (and a year younger) than Lockhart, tried to outdo one another in spectacular onslaughts upon their contemporaries. The *Edinburgh Review* was in the pleasant position of attacking the Tory government in power at the time, and all that pertained thereto. The wits of *Blackwood* must attack persons.

Though the conclusions expressed here were arrived at a dozen years before he wrote, I am happy to find them substantiated by the latest writer on Lockhart. Dr. Gilbert Macbeth in his *J. G. Lockhart, a Critical Study* (Urbana, University of Illinois Press, 1935), 207–208, concludes that his subject possessed "tolerance and balance" even in his early years of association with *Maga.*

The truth is that his contributions to *Blackwood's* of an objectionable sort constitute a very small proportion of the mass of his writings for that periodical. Furthermore, his treatment of Hunt and his group, the *Edinburgh* reviewers, and the others who felt his sting, reflects very little upon his intellectual caliber, whatever may be its bearing upon his quality as a man. In our study of these phases of his career, it was evident that the controlling factor was an exigency of the moment, i.e., the success of the magazine; and that it was his boyish love of sensation, and, paradoxically, the very excellence of his intellectual endowment, that compelled him to go to undue lengths. . . .

In the summing up of Lockhart's career, one aspect of it is sure to attract the notice of the reader—the contrast between his early promise and his actual achievement. . . . Apart from biography, his literary history practically comes to an end at about the age of thirty, an age at which many writers, and critics in particular, are just beginning to find themselves.

After pointing out that Lockhart's temperament was intellectual rather than creative, Dr. Macbeth continues:

He has been blamed for continuing to write for *Blackwood's* in spite of the insults of his enemies and the admonitions of Scott. The fact is that he could not find anything better to do. During the *Blackwood's* period he wrote four novels, doubtless in a vain endeavor to find a new field of activity and be thereby in a position to cut himself clear of the magazine. There is plenty of evidence that he rebelled against the slavery of journalism, and that he tried to escape it by leaving literature entirely; to him the world of affairs always seemed the only world of real consequence. But he could not escape.

In *Notes and Queries,* since 1943, I have been publishing selections from the more than one thousand letters which Lockhart wrote Croker between 1819 and 1854. As introduction to the correspondence between the two in May and June, 1821—treated in the next section—it may be remarked here that between 1819 and 1821 Croker and Lockhart were on cordial if not personally intimate terms. The Irishman first wrote the Scotsman on November 18, 1819, seeking assistance for a new Tory weekly, the *Constitution*—later renamed the *Guardian*—a rickety bantling that died slowly between the end of December, 1819, and April, 1824. Lockhart sent various contributions to this paper from Scotland in 1819 and 1820. Perhaps he first met Croker personally when he hurried to London in January, 1821, to challenge John Scott for the attacks directed upon himself in the *London Magazine*. Three letters, the first simply dated "Admiralty one o'clock" and the second "5 o'clock Admiralty," show that Lockhart sought out Croker immediately after reaching London. By way of footnote it may be added that after his antagonist's departure to Edinburgh, John Scott renewed the warfare in the press; and (thanks to a couple of amateur seconds) at Chalk Farm at 9 p.m. on February 16, 1821, by the light of the moon, J. H. Christie, Lockhart's friend at Oxford, after firing once in the air, shot and fatally wounded Scott.

In May, 1821, Croker was forty years old, a successful man of the world, capable and self-assured: a steady conservative and already a bulwark of the Tory government —ready within a dozen years to best Macaulay in their tilts on the Reform Bill in the House of Commons, increasingly indispensable to the Admiralty and increasingly indispensable also to John Murray as a contributor to the *Quarterly Review* on politics, and, however limited esthetically, on literature in general, especially belles-lettres. In May, 1821, Lockhart was not quite twenty-seven, an elegant young man with black curly hair and a splendid eye—shy, sarcastic, socially exclusive, with a first class in Classics as a Snell fellow of Balliol behind him, and no professional future whatever before him, except, as has been shown, a connection since 1817 with *Blackwood's Magazine.* Croker's personal life had been permanently saddened by the loss of his three-year-old son on May 15, 1820; and Lockhart's had been clouded by John Scott's death in February, 1821. Only because of his connection with another Scott was he chosen editor of the *Quarterly Review* within the next five years.

4. Proof of the Authorship

A Letter to the Right Hon. Lord Byron by John Bull was published in pamphlet form in May or late April, 1821. Curiously, Byron himself admired the piece. "I have just read 'John Bull's letter'; it is diabolically *well* written, and full of fun and ferocity. I must forgive the dog, whoever he is."[34] More restrainedly Scott wrote Lord Montagu:

> Pray have you seen John Bulls Letter to Lord Byron if not I think it will entertain you. It has much . . . cool assurance and . . . cleverness. . . . Croker of course falls under general and I think deserved suspicion. The trade is something perilous.[35]

That Lockhart was the author I have shown in the *London Times Literary Supplement* for November 30, 1940, from which I now quote.

Professor Samuel C. Chew writes in *Byron in England* (p. 39): "Praise of *Don Juan* of another sort is contained in a pamphlet which is by far the most interesting of all contemporary bits of Byroniana, and is the only one

[34] *The Works of Lord Byron: Letters and Journals,* ed. by R. E. Prothero (London, John Murray, 1922, 7 vols.), V, 315–16; hereafter referred to as Byron, *Letters and Journals.*

[35] Grierson (ed.), *Letters of Scott 1819–1821,* VI, 448–49.

which, I believe, is worth reprinting. This is *A Letter to the Right Hon. Lord Byron. By John Bull* [London, Wright], 1821." In a note Professor Chew considers the authorship of this brochure: "The knowledge of Edinburgh and of Scotch literature shown in it; the knowledge of German, and the good command of the classics all point to John Black of the staff of the *Morning Chronicle.*" All three virtues noted are especially attributable to Lockhart; and some unpublished letters of Lockhart and Croker, which the William L. Clements Library of the University of Michigan courteously allows me to publish, definitely establish his having written the piece.

As an introduction to the six letters from the Clements Library (seven, if the letter from Croker to Murray is counted), hitherto unprinted letter from Croker to Lockhart, included here by permission of the National Library of Scotland has great interest.

CROKER TO LOCKHART

Confidential

May 17. 1821

My dear Mr. Lockhart

They have sent me today a very able "letter of J Bull to Lord Byron" & they tell me it is *yours.* I believe them, for it is spirited, witty & just—but for heaven's sake, why narrow & impair your utility by avowing it—perhaps you do not *avow* it & think I have been told a *secret,* but it has not been told to me as such—altho' I shall certainly keep it as one—but I would beg of you in any thing of the same kind hereafter to recollect that any good you can do will be exactly proportioned to the impenetrability of your mask—

The *John Bull* newspaper had lost much of its effect by being attributed to me but when folks found out that I really

LORD BYRON

From a sketch by Count D'Orsay
made in May, 1823

Edinburgh
May 21.

Confidential

My dear Sir I feel very very much obliged to you — but was never more surprised than by your letter. I will not indeed deny to you that I wrote that letter but how I who have been accused or even suspicted I cannot for my life divine. & so far from avowing it I promise you I w^d pay a tremendous fine rather than bear the blame of it for a week.

I place in you the most implicit reliance in your friendliness. I pray you to do everything in your power to stop the report if it be a report. I cannot imagine how it has arisen — but I am quite sure nobody has any knowledge of the thing — My only suspicion is that Murray has extracted from Wright (what he promised in writing & conceal most sacredly) the name of the agent thro' whom the thing was sent to him. Of my part Mr Wright has no knowledge

Do let me hear that it is at an end. and I shall be greatly relieved.

Very faithfully yours
J G Lockhart.

I cannot say how much I am distressed with this thing — not on my own account God knows — but on Scott's. For I wrote the thing when in Inverness shire & he has never heard of it. I hope never will. Do say whatever is strongest & most effectual to save me from a great pain. I am a most unfortunate fellow —

Lockhart's letter to Croker, May 21, 1821

From a photostat reproduced by permission of the William L. Clements Library, Ann Arbor

had nothing to do with it, it became powerful again—in the same way Byron's John Bull would lose half its force & spirit if *any* name be affixed to him.

Excuse this hint which a sincere regard for you & an interest in all you do prompts.

Yours faithfully
J W Croker

The letters from the Clements Library follow.

LOCKHART TO CROKER

confidential

Edinburgh May 21 [1821]

My dear Sir

I feel *very very* much obliged to you—but was never more surprised than by your letter. I will not indeed deny *to you* that I wrote that letter but how I shd have been accused or even suspected I cannot for my life divine. & so far frm avowing it I promise you I wd pay a tremendous fine rather than bear the blame of it for a week.

I place as you see the most implicit reliance on your friendliness. I *pray* you do everything *in your power* to stop the report if it be a report. I cannot imagine how it has arisen —but I am quite sure nobody has any *knowledge* of the thing. My only suspicion is that Murray has extracted frm *Wright* (what *he* promised in initio to conceal most sacredly) the name of the agent thro' whom the thing was sent to him. Of my part Mr Wright has no knowledge.

Do let me hear that it is at an end and I shall be greatly relieved.

Very faithfully yours
JGLockhart

I cannot say how much I am disturbed with this thing —not on my own account God knows—but on *Scott's*. For I wrote the thing when in Inverness shire & he has never heard of it. I hope never will. Do say whatever is strongest & most effectual to save me frm a great pain. I am a most impractical fellow. [I have written Murray to deny the letter *crossed out by Lockhart.*] No I have not written Murray I trust everything *to you.*

CROKER TO LOCKHART

confidential

24 May 1821

My dear Sir

There can be no doubt that Mr Wright has betrayed your *name* most idly and unjustifiably—nay I think I heard from Murray that he said that the pamphlet had not been printed in London but had been sent from Edinburgh and I think there was some mention of *Scott's* having been the channel of communication. I shall contradict the report: but my means of contradiction are very limited. I think you might write a *thunderer* to Mr Wright and oblige him to contradict his assertion, for you may depend upon it that the report came from him, and I heard it from more than one. I know nothing of Mr Wright but it would seem that he is a babbling sort of man who by some means or other guesses you to be the author, and to do honor to his own judgment has told it in *confidence* to every one who would listen to him.

Murray has just lost his child. I will tell him when I see him of your disclaimer—but it seems to me that Mr Wright should be obliged to retract his own improper and groundless reports. As Murray is not visible I cannot tell to whom *Wright* told the thing, but I have no doubt that he did so to some one who told Murray. I think he said his printer.

Yours ever

JWC.

P.S. I have written to Murray* to say that I had mentioned Bull's letter to you and that you have answered me in utter *ignorance* and *astonishment,* so that he may look elsewhere for the author.

24 May 1821

*Dear Murray

You will believe that I can pity you and Mrs Murray, but I have known too well the folly of all condolence to attempt it with you: but in comparing your case with my own I see how incomparably less dreadful your loss is than that which has broken *our* hearts and blasted *our* hopes.

I had mentioned to Mr Lockhart that I had heard that *he* was the author of John Bull he answered me in utter ignorance and astonishment. He has never heard of the letter and knows nothing about it. Therefore we must look elsewhere for the author—if indeed it be worth while to look about for an author who ranks Pope and Coleridge together.

Do you remember my *writing* to you (I think I *wrote*) some years ago that I thought Lord Byron's genius essentially dramatic and tragic. Mr Bull it seems supports the same opinion; but it happens to be the only one in which I concur with him unless indeed his contempt of Bowles for it may I suppose be called *contempt* that I have never read a line of that elegant poet.

Yours etc.
JWC.

LOCKHART TO CROKER

private

My dear Sir:

I am much distressed with Master Wrights folly and impudence. Having seen his name on the New Whig Guide Tentamen[36] &c I had vent[ur]ed to form an idea of him which proves to be lamentably incorrect

I have written him a letter which I think must frighten

36 Tentamen; or, an Essay towards the History of Whittington, some time Lord Mayor of London; by Vicesimus Blinkinsop [Theodore Hook], *LL.D. F.R.S. A.S.S. &c &c*—"Monthly List of New Publications," *Blackwood's Magazine,* September, 1820, 696.

him and shall hope to hear of the reports final destruction and death very soon meantime believe me once more

Your most obliged
JGLockhart

Edinburgh
May 28 [1821]

CROKER TO LOCKHART

31 May 1821

My dear Sir

I have heard and I believe the report, that Mr Wright only reported what he had himself heard from Edinburgh and that he in his own defence has shown a letter from *your* printer in Edinburgh, *mentioning your name as the author of the letter.* If this be the fact it is clear that the imprudence has taken place nearer home than was at first supposed.

Observe that I am but superficially informed on the subject as I can only tell you what I hear in cursory conversation with Murray and such like, as I have no acquaintance with Mr Wright of whom I know nothing, and of whom I do not think it likely I ever shall. At all events I am really sorry to tell you that I have no doubt that you will be considered as the author in spite of any thing you may do; for, as I have said, there is a *litera scripta* from the best authority at Edinburgh against you.

Yours &c
JWC

LOCKHART TO CROKER

My dear Sir

I have been in the country for several days or your letter had not lain unanswered. I can *only* say that the letter was printed in *London* I know not by whom—so that it is impossible the report you mention shd have any foundation in fact. I enclose you Wrights answer to my letter frm which you will see how perfectly *he* is or pretends to be in the dark. I understand he has written Murray to the same effect but if so you have probably heard of it. Once more very faithfully yours

JG Lockhart

If you can suggest anything further to be done I pray you do so
Edinburgh
June 7th 1821

CROKER TO LOCKHART

14 June 1821

My dear Sir

I return Mr Wright's letter. I can only say that a gentleman told me that he *had seen* a letter from Mr Blackwood to Mr Wright stating you to be the author of the letter.

I have not myself seen Blackwood's letter nor do I know of any of the parties to the publication, but I was startled at receiving the pamphlet with your name written in the title page, and this led me to enquire into the fact and write you as I did.

I am &c
JWC.

In *Blackwood's Magazine* of July, 1821, an article, "Letter to Lord Byron," fathers John Bull's letter upon Jeremy Bentham! According to it, various ladies accused of reading *Don Juan* have written indignant denials, including a Mrs. Goddard:

> "Little I thought the wide world was to hear o' me,
> All through the means of you, Mr. Jeremy;
> Never a woman, I'm sure, was more bother'd, sir,
> Than your humble servant, I, Mrs. Goddard, sir," &c.

The article ridicules Bentham's supposed pamphlet

throughout and compares with it *Maga's* own treatment of the poet:

> Of our castigation of Don Juan, we are proud, and laugh at the vaporings of Lord Byron, who says he will answer us. If he do, we shall annihilate him in the twinkling of a bed-post.

To mystify the public, to set up a smoke screen protecting Lockhart by accusing the Whig Bentham of writing the pamphlet, is typical of the *Blackwood* group! and may be added to their other numerous japes in these early years of *Maga*.

Croker lied like a gentleman—and Lockhart, who had written "by far the most interesting of all contemporary bits of Byroniana," spent an evil three weeks regretting his sin and never acknowledged his epistolary critical masterpiece. A discovery might, indeed, have affected his life. If John Murray had known the authorship, would he, four and one-half years later, have signed the agreement making Lockhart editor of the *Quarterly Review* on October 20, 1825?

5. Lockhart on Byron

Lockhart under the alias "Wastle" contributed the first installment of his poem, the *Mad Banker of Amsterdam,* to *Blackwood's Magazine* of July and August, 1818 (with continuations in February and March, 1819, and January, 1820). This poem, written in the ottava rima, after the manner of Byron's *Beppo,* has something of the breeziness and amateurish spontaneity of *Don Juan.* Lang in his *Life of Lockhart* quotes stanzas twenty-five and twenty-six of the fifth canto with approval, but I feel that in this serious invective—"Alas for Jeffrey!"—"Wastle" merely stridulates, and that he is far more successful in stanza thirteen, where he retains his ballast of humor:

> Or Jeffrey, with his front so full of witticisms,
> Unconscious quite of that organization,
> Scribbling what fawning fools misnomer criticisms,
> Against the spirits of majestic station.
> He should have stuck to side-bar quirks and petty schisms,
> For deuce a pile has he of *veneration.*
> Heavens! what a gulf impassable doth sever
> Wits from the wise—the great man from the clever!
>
> —IV, 564.

That Lockhart was acquainted with *Beppo* appears from some remarks he makes in *Peter's Letters to His Kinsfolk* of 1819, where, defending an article in *Blackwood's Magazine* of June, 1818, he writes:

> Another letter, addressed about the same time to Lord Byron on the publication of his Beppo, was meanly and stupidly represented by the enemies of the magazine as a malignant attack on this great poet; whereas it is, in truth, filled, from beginning to end, with marks of the most devout admiration for his genius, and bears every appearance of having been written with the sincere desire to preserve that majestic genius from being degraded, by wasting its inspirations on themes of an immoral or unworthy description.—II, 217.

In this same *Peter's Letters to His Kinsfolk,* Lockhart says that he never met Byron. In a passing reference he contrasts the love poetry of Coleridge and Byron: Coleridge's

> love-poetry is, throughout, the finest that has been produced in England since the days of Shakespeare and the old dramatists. Lord Byron represents the passion of love with a power and fervor every way worthy of his genius, but he does not

seem to understand the nature of the feeling which these old English poets called by the name of Love. His love is entirely oriental: the love of haughty warriors reposing on the bosom of humble slaves, swallowed up in the unquestioning potency of a passion, imbibed in, and from the very sense of, their perpetual inferiority.—II, 220–21.

In a later Letter, dealing with Craniology, Lockhart contrasts the heads of Byron, Scott, and others: "Lord Byron's head is, without doubt, the finest in our time" (II, 338).

In Appendix A will be found an outline of Byron's treatment in *Blackwood's Magazine.* There are shown Lockhart's articles in relation to the articles of his colleagues: as will appear, he assisted Maginn in the most violent of the attacks on *Don Juan* in July, 1823: he wrote, alone, the most laudatory review of the poem in September, 1823. Professor Paul G. Trueblood, who has made a study of estimates of *Don Juan* in British contemporary periodicals, refers thus to the latter piece:

This review, appearing in a Tory journal, is one of the few examples of veritable literary criticism of *Don Juan* produced in Byron's day.

Dr. Trueblood says of Lockhart's article of September, 1823, and Jeffrey's article on "Lord Byron's Tragedies" of February, 1822:

These two reviews, one by Francis Jeffrey in a Whig journal and the other by William Maginn [*should be* J. G. Lockhart] in a Tory journal, stand out like oases in a sterile desert of critical prejudice.[37]

But nine months before ever Jeffrey wrote his article, there appeared Lockhart's *Letter to Byron on Don Juan,* which, under its insolent tone, shows a true appreciation

37 Trueblood, *The Flowering of Byron's Genius,* 64, 73.

of the author's authentic greatness. Wordsworth in 1798 was welcomed by almost universal silence; Byron a little more than twenty years later was welcomed by an almost unanimity of hisses. At a time when the Respectable World was heaving its hands heavenward in horror at *Don Juan,* an unknown youngster of twenty-six proclaimed the power of this greatest of English epic satires.

In the *Letter to Byron on Don Juan,* Lockhart after having read the first three cantos, advises Byron

> to bring the Don forthwith into England—to put him to school at Harrow, and to college at Cambridge,—to lodge him at the Clarendon, and make him see the world,—as you yourself have seen it,—and describe it as Sir Walter Scott has described Captain Clutterbuck.

Byron's plan for the poem was very elastic. He jocosely informed Murray on April 6, 1819, that he will write fifty cantos; and on August 12, 1819, he informs him: "You ask me for the plan of Donny Johnny: I *have* no plan. . . . Why, man, the Soul of such writing is its licence." But before he had received Lockhart's advice in April or May, 1821, he had planned that his hero should visit England, as appears in a famous outline of the poem in his letter to John Murray of February 16, 1821:

> The 5th is so far from being the last of *D. J.,* that it is hardly the beginning. I meant to take him the tour of Europe, with a proper mixture of siege, battle, and adventure, and to make him finish as *Anacharsis Cloots* in the French revolution. To how many cantos this may extend, I know not . . . but this was my notion: I meant to have made him a *Cavalier Servente* in Italy, and the cause of a divorce in England, and a Sentimental "Werther-faced man" in Germany, so as to show the different ridicules of the society in each of these countries.[38]

[38] Byron, *Letters and Journals,* IV, 284, 342; V, 242.

LETTER

TO THE

RIGHT HON. LORD BYRON.

BY JOHN BULL.

Some of Bull's friends advised him to take gentle methods with the young Lord; but John naturally loved rough play.—

It is impossible to express the surprise of LORD STRUTT upon the receipt of this Letter.

ARBUTHNOT.

LONDON:

PRINTED BY AND FOR WILLIAM WRIGHT, FLEET-STREET.

1821.

The following Letter is the First of a Series, to be continued occasionally. The Second Letter is addressed to Mr. Thomas Campbell. The Third to His Majesty the King. And the Fourth is also to Lord Byron.[2]

---

1 The quotation on the preceding title page is from John Arbuthnot, *The History of John Bull* (London, 1774), 21.

2 There is no record of a continuation of the series.

LETTER,

&c. &c.

MY LORD,

IN a very late publication[3] you remark, almost with the air of a discoverer, that "in fact, the great *primum mobile* of the present age is *cant;*"[4] and then you proceed in prose, much better than, I honestly tell you, I ever thought you could have written, to illustrate this position by sundry very excellent detections of the *cant* of the Bowleses.[5] Your Lordship is very right in what you say about *cant,* but if it really was your object to prove that it is the *primum mobile* in the literature of our day, why, in the world, did you take the Bowleses for your illustration? If the literature of the present age could find a convenient organ by which to address itself to the

3 *Letter to John Murray, Esqre, on the Rev. W. L. Bowles's Strictures on the Life and Writings of Pope,* March, 1821; Byron, *Letters and Journals,* V, 536–66.

4 The actual statement is, "The truth is, that in these days the grand '*primum mobile*' of England is *cant;* cant political, cant poetical, cant religious, cant moral; but always *cant,* multiplied through al the varieties of life."—*Ibid.,* 542.

5 William Lisle Bowles (1762–1850) issued a ten-volume edition of Pope, with an introduction containing a sketch of Pope's life and strictures on his poetry. Bowles maintained that "images from nature are more sublime than images from art." Byron took great exception to Bowles's comments—*Dictionary of National Biography.* (Hereafter notes, unless otherwise explained, come from this series of volumes.)

Bowleses, its language would be *τιε μοι και ὑμιν*;[6] the fact is, that *cant* IS the *primum mobile;* but the Bowleses are not among the *mota* over which this *momentum* exerts any extraordinary influence. Not even *cant* can set them a rolling up the hill: others are more fortunate. The true question is, whether, even in regard to these *cant* will not in the end prove to be a sorry *primum mobile* of the Sisyphon school[7] after all? And it is in this view of the subject that I feel induced to trouble your Lordship with a few plain observations upon *cant,* or, as I shall call it, for the sake of sweet variety, my Lord, HUMBUG.

I say that I shall call it so for the sake of sweet variety: chiefly so, certainly; and yet, I think, the word is *per se* the better and more expressive word of the two. I have my reasons for thinking so, and I shall give you them by-and-bye. But, in the mean time, I have no hesitation in avowing my suspicion that, "in fact,"[8] the two words are not at all synonyms. I think I can see an essential difference between the thing *cant* and the thing *humbug;* but it may be but a delusion of mine after all. I do think, however, and that is enough for our present purpose, that Cant is the more solemn, grave, steady variety; Humbug the more airy. Cant is the high German Doctor, (no allusion to the great Immanuel Kant of Kœnigsberg[9]) who carries the whole thing through with the same imperturbable face of stupid hypocrisy. Humbug, again, I recognise in the Merry Andrew, who grins at his elbow, and

6 What is this to you and me?

7 In *English Bards and Scotch Reviewers,* lines 411–17, Byron compares the mental labors of one Maurice with the labors of Sisyphus.

8 See the garbled quotation, p. 63.

9 Immanuel Kant (1724–1804) was a German metaphysician. Lockhart was particularly well versed in German philosophy and critical theories.—Lang, *Life of Lockhart,* I, 171.

only now and then condescends to ape the gravity of your true cant. Cant eats more than humbug; humbug drinks more than cant: cant is soured through and through; humbug is a jolly devil at heart. But why use many words when a single example will make the matter as clear as moonshine? Leaving periphrasis to the *Cantabs,*[10] I am of opinion, once for all, that such a man as Mr. Wilberforce[11] is a living type of *cant.* Your Lordship will easily understand my meaning when I say that Lord Byron answers more exactly to my idea of the man of HUMBUG.

Do not imagine, however, that I have either *cant* or *humbug* enough about me to attempt persuading people that you are nothing but humbug, as Mr. Wilberforce is nothing but cant. That would not go down either with the public or with you, or with myself: while the truth will make itself to be swallowed, if not to be relished, by all the three. But, before proceeding to the general subject, perhaps the better way may be to begin with a short sketch of what I conceive to be the true opinion entertained concerning my Lord Byron by himself, and by all other people of sense and discrimination.

I think then, in the first place, that nobody dreams of disputing your Lordship's claims to be considered as a great and masterly poet. Few even of the most abject disciples of Humbug go so far as to hint any doubts as to that matter. There are, indeed, two or three that do and

10 Lockhart attended Oxford; Byron was a Cambridge man.

11 William Wilberforce (1759–1833) led a movement for the abolition of the slave trade. In *Don Juan,* Canto IV, stanza 115, Byron mentions Wilberforce:

> Twelve negresses from Nubia brought a price
> Which the West Indian market scarce could bring,
> Though Wilberforce, at last, has made it twice
> What 'twas ere Abolition.

have done so; but every body laughs at them. There is, for example, a most lumbering Goth[12] in the Literary Gazette,[13] who has been trying to prove that you are the most extensive and the most impudent of plagiarists.[14] In order to establish this, he proves against your Lordship about the five-hundredth part of what might be proved by any man of the smallest learning against any one poet born since the death of Homer; and of what any man of sense living in Homer's time (if indeed there ever was any such person as Homer) could, I doubt not, have proved with equal success against old Homer himself. Two things, however, there are, which this Theban[15] has proved in a most satisfactory manner indeed: and these are his own base ignorance, and his still baser envy. It is clear that your adversary has never read almost any poetry at all; for he blames your Lordship most bitterly for copying things from Scott, Wordsworth, and so forth, which any boarding-school miss that has read the Elegant Extracts[16] could have told him had been copied by them from the English poets of the two preceding centuries—which any Eton lad, again, could have traced to Greek

12 Alaric A. Watts (1797–1864) contributed to *Blackwood's Magazine*. The *Blackwood* group pretended to think the initial *A,* which in reality stood for "Alexander," stood for "Attila"; hence "the Goth."—Mrs. Oliphant, *Annals of a Publishing House,* I, 209.

13 A weekly journal of belles-lettres, founded by William Jerdan in 1817 and edited by him until 1850.

14 Watts contributed to the *Literary Gazette* a series of papers called "Borrowings from Byron," February–March, 1821. Commenting on these papers, Byron wrote Tom Moore, "I think I now, in my time, have been accused of *every* thing."—Byron, *Letters and Journals,* V, 336.

15 The mad Lear called Edgar, who was feigning madness, the "learned Theban."—Shakespeare, *King Lear,* III: 4: 162.

16 *Elegant Extracts, or Useful and Entertaining Pieces of Poetry, selected for the improvement of Youth,* compiled by Vicesimus Knox (1752–1821) and first published anonymously in London in 1789.

and Latin—and any puppy that has spent a year beyond the Alps would have taken a pleasure in showing him, over and over again, embalmed in that beautiful dialect, of whose beauty no English writer (since Gray) appears to have had the real feeling but yourself. I say nothing of the absurdity of the whole idea. There was a man, as you know, (though our Goth does not,) who tried to persuade the world that Sterne had stolen all his wit from Burton.[17] One thousand and one attempts have been made of the same kind long ago, and forgotten; and here is one more which will be forgotten in due time, that is to say, in another week. So much for his ignorance: his envy, it is more difficult to understand. Your Lordship writes for the LITERARY WORLD,[18] and he writes for the LITERARY GAZETTE; and both of you are accepted. What would the man have? Is he not satisfied with his elevation? Is he already like the Macedonian, sighing for new conquests? Oh! most insatiable and irrational of appetites, thy name is *ambition!*

And yet this is not the only person who has questioned, in one way or another, your Lordship's title to be considered as a great and original poet. There are the Lakers,[19] my Lord; aye, the whole school of Glaramara and Skiddaw and Dunmailraise, who have the vanity to be in

17 John Ferriar (1761–1815) in his *Illustrations of Sterne,* 1798, traced the obligations of Laurence Sterne (1713–68) in *Tristam Shandy* to the *Anatomy of Melancholy* by Robert Burton (1577–1640). Ferriar's intention, however, was merely to illustrate his author rather than to convict him of plagiarism.

18 *The Union List of Serials in Libraries of the United States and Canada,* ed. by Winifred Gregory (New York, H. W. Wilson Company, 1943), lists no such periodical. It is likely that Lockhart meant "the public."

19 Byron called them "Wordsworth and Co."—*The Works of Lord Byron: Poetry,* ed. by Ernest Hartley Coleridge (London, John Murray, 1918–24, 7 vols.), IV, 182 n. 1; hereafter referred to as Byron, *Poetry.*

the habit of undervaluing your poetical talents. Mr. Southey[20] thinks you would never have thought of going over the sea had it not been for his Thalaba [1801]; Mr. Wordsworth[21] is humbly of opinion that no man in the world ever thought a tree beautiful, or a mountain grand, till he announced his own wonderful perceptions. Mr. Charles Lambe thinks you would never have written Beppo [1818] had he not joked, nor Lara [1814][22] had he not sighed. Mr. Lloyd half suspects your Lordship has read his Nugæ Canoræ [1819]: now all these fancies are alike ridiculous, and you are well entitled to laugh as much as you please at them, and those who hold them. But there is one Laker who praises your Lordship,—and why? Because your Lordship praised him. This is Coleridge, who, on the strength of a little compliment in one of your bad notes,[23] (for your notes are all bad,) ventured at last to open to the gaze of day the long secluded loveliness of Christabelle [1816],—and with what effect his

20 "Lockhart and Southey never 'took to' each other. Of all faults Lockhart most detested *vanity*."—Lang, *Life of Lockhart,* II, 274.

21 Lang says, "As early as 1825, Lockhart had laughed at the sage's self-absorption and total disregard of the merits of his great contemporaries." —*Ibid.,* II, 336. Lockhart seems to have detected Wordsworth's foibles somewhat earlier—perhaps through conversations with John Wilson. Actually, however, Lockhart did have a true appreciation of Wordsworth's genius.

22 In 1815 Lockhart wrote his friend Christie: "You underrate Lord Byron, I think. 'Lara' I look upon as a wonderful production."—*Ibid.,* I, 70.

23 The note was to *The Siege of Corinth,* stanza 19, lines 521–32. Byron acknowledged that these lines bore a resemblance to a passage in the then unpublished *Christabel* but claimed that at the time they were written he had not "heard that wild and singularly original and beautiful poem recited; and the MS. of that production I never saw till very recently, by the kindness of Mr. Coleridge himself. . . . Let me conclude by a hope that he will not longer delay the publication of a production, of which I can only add my mite of approbation to the applause of far more competent judges."—Byron, *Poetry,* III, 471.

bookseller doth know.[24] Poor Coleridge, however, although his pamphlet would not sell, still gloated over the puff, and he gave your Lordship, in return, a great many very reasonable good puffs[25] in prose, both rhymed and un-rhymed, of the merits of which your Lordship has not, I am very sorry to observe, expressed any thing like a decent sense. You may do very well to quiz Wordsworth for his vanity, and Southey for his pompousness; but what right have you to say any thing about Mr. Coleridge's drinking? Really, my Lord, I have no scruple in saying, that I look upon that line of yours—"Coleridge is drunk," &c.[26] as quite personal—shamefully personal. As Coleridge never saw Don Juan, or if he did, forgot the whole affair next morning, it is nothing in regard to him; but what can be expected from his friends? Has not any one of them (if he has any) a perfect right, after reading that line, to print and publish, if he pleases, all that all the world has heard about your Lordship's own life and conversation? And if any one of them should do so, what would you, my Lord Byron, think of it? It is easy for you to say that you despise abuse. But this would not be abuse,—it would merely be justice. It would amount to nothing more than a detection of the operation of your Lordship's *primum mobile,* which, to do your Lordship justice, is not, I believe, HUMBUG, however near it may come, in one sense, to CANT.

By the Lakers, then, take them as a body,— (Words-

[24] John Murray published *Christabel* upon a specific recommendation from Byron. Financially the poem was a failure.

[25] Chew in commenting on this passage says: "To what can this refer? Coleridge never 'puffed' Byron."—*Byron in England,* 40, n. 1.

[26] Canto I, stanza 205 of *Don Juan* reads in part:

> Thou shalt not set up Wordsworth, Coleridge, Southey;
> Because the first is crazed beyond all hope,
> The second drunk, the third so quaint and mouthy.

worth, perhaps, would suggest "take them as a soul,")—you are abused: but I pray you not to be overmuch cast down. Let not your heart be discomfited within you, neither let it be afraid. In the Lakers' house of scorn there are many mansions;[27] and your Lordship can scarcely need to be informed, that you inhabit but one of them. "In fact," to use your Lordship's happy anti-humbug phrase, the Lakers are not understood to be much in the habit of giving good—very good words—to any one beyond their own sweet circle. Read their notes. I know this is asking a considerable favour; yet, if it were but for the sake of humbug, do read them. You will then perceive, as all that have read them already have done,—that "in fact" the Lakers would fain have us believe there are no poets in the world but themselves,—or, at least, that they (again taking them as a body) are a first without a second. Find me out, if you can, one simple, downright, direct, honest, word of commendation bestowed by any one of all these poets (true or *soi-disants*) upon any one contemporary poet who never drank tea infused with the water of Winander-mere, "mine own sweet lake."[28] They have all lived with Scott, for example, and they *must* all know what Scott is; yet where in any of all their books do we find one single sentence of just tribute to the most original (I am sure *you* won't quarrel with that epithet) if not the most exquisite genius of our age? No such thing: where can you see them—any one of them—quoting *him,* as they, one and all, do, *usque ad nauseam,* each other? No, no; you will not find Wordsworth quoting Scott, (no, not although Scott—good easy man, has often quoted

27 John 14:27, and a parody of John 14:2.

28 "Our own dear lake" occurs in stanza 10 of Byron's *Epistle to Augusta,* written in 1816 but not published until 1830.

Wordsworth,[29])—nor will you find the Poet Laureate quoting Scott, (no, not even although but for him he never would have been Poet Laureate,[30])—nor will you find Charles Lambe quoting Scott, (although the verses of that respectable clerk in the India House stand in about the same relation to the verses of the Northern Minstrel, in which the bleatings of a real yearling might have done to the neighings of the war-horse of Charlemagne:) nor will you find even the Lloyds themselves doing any such thing—for even the Lloyds are Lakers—and, as such, intolerant vanity sits, and must ever sit, like some enormous nightmare, on their bosoms. This letter is written on the anti-humbug principle: so why should the truth be concealed? The truth very shortly and very simply is, that these gentlemen have been making such a noise in their own ears, with their own penny trumpets, that they have heard little or nothing of the music over which all the world beyond Glaramara has been hanging enamoured. Ask a Laker, in private, what he thinks of Scott. I bet you Marmion [1808] to the Excursion [1814][31]—nay, I bet you the Antiquary [1816]—the answer will be—"Oh, very well! very well indeed! My friend, Mr. Scott,—I beg his pardon, I mean Sir Walter, is a very pleasant, and, upon my honour, I tell ye the truth, a very clever gentleman. But, as for poetry, imagination, nature," (oh, that you could hear the Glaramara method

29 For example, on the title page of *Rob Roy,* Scott quotes some lines of *Rob Roy's Grave*. Lockhart probably refers, however, to oral quotation.

30 Scott refused an offer of the Laureateship, suggesting that it be bestowed on Southey, who accepted it in 1813.

31 Of *The Excursion* Lockhart said, "I enjoyed it deeply."—Lang, *Life of Lockhart,* I, 102. Byron's well-known lines in *Don Juan,* Canto III, stanza 94, run:

> A drowsy frowzy poem, call'd the "Excursion,"
> Writ in a manner which is my aversion.

of pronouncing such words as these!) "why I need not say what I think: for that you know is not the part of a friend." A pause would ensue, and then the magnanimous Laker would, without doubt, vouchsafe to read you a little bit from some MS. of his own, which he or his wife would tell you, with a knowing look, had lain in his desk ever since the era of the French revolution.

Now, this is very well in its way: and yet it is nothing to their treatment of you. In their talk, as I hear, they affect, my Lord, (for observe it is all humbug,) to consider you as a person of very ordinary talents indeed, and withal, a great reprobate; which last, if it be so, is a thing they are no judges of, and have nothing whatever to do with. In all their books and pamphlets, however, you will seek in vain for even the most distant allusion to your name: and yet, in the said books and pamphlets, they are by no means shy of quotation or of alluding to names. Their principal favourites "in fact," (I mean in the way of allusion and quotation,) are very obscure fifth-rate persons,—Withers, for example, and other forgotten poetasters,—the whole of whose works are not worth five couplets of any one of your Lordship's poems. In quoting from and praising such people as these, they do not injure their own cast (for I think the forgotten dead and the neglected living may not unfairly be considered as of the same cast:) but one word of praise bestowed on you, whom the world has praised, would be a sort of acknowledgement that the world has some perceptions, and would therefore infer not a slight sarcasm against themselves. This is so plain, that there is no need for enlarging upon it; and nothing can be more manifest than that these people have acted amiss towards you.

And yet, admitting all these things, I am of opinion

that you have acted still more amiss towards them. The world has neglected them, my Lord, and, if they be a little more sore and thin-skinned than is usual among men of any sense, the treatment they have met with ought really to be accepted as affording some excuse for their frailties. You and I may have a right to laugh at them in private: but what right had the Jeffreys[32] *et hoc genus omne* to laugh at them in public? There can be no question the lines have not fallen to the Lakers in pleasant places. I, for my part, don't care a farthing about being laughed at, and nobody will dispute your Lordship's right to say, in the words of the adage, *"Homme qui rit n'est pas dangereux."* But how could poor Wordsworth say so? and observe, I don't use the word *poor* as a mere Homeric epithet,—for "in fact" the laughter of the Jeffreys kept Wordsworth poor, miserably poor for twenty years, and *poor* he would have continued on to this blessed day, "dwelling retired in his simplicity,"[33] but for my good Lord of Lonsdale, and the tax-collectorship, from which the great Laker has derived the name by which he is now best known all over the Glaramara region, I mean, that of the STAMP-MASTER; and, if he be as harsh a tax-gatherer as he is a critic, *certes!* the great William Wordsworth must be a great bore, and curses not loud but deep must be daily echoed by

"All that ancient brotherhood of hills!"[34]

32 Critics such as Francis Jeffrey, editor of the Whig *Edinburgh Review,* who was condescendingly hostile toward Wordsworth. Lockhart said in *Peter's Letters to His Kinsfolk* that the *Edinburgh Review* offered "a diet of levity and sarcastic indifference."—quoted in Lang, *Life of Lockhart,* I, 149.

33 "Dwelling retired in our simplicity."—W. Wordsworth, *To Joanna,* line 10.

34 "A work accomplished by the brotherhood
Of ancient mountains, . . ."—*Ibid.,* lines 69–70.

But to return to your Lordship, (not that I am done with the stamp-master,)—all the world then agree with yourself in thinking you a great poet,—those only excepted whom the most egregious vanity hath hoodwinked, doth hoodwink, and ever will hoodwink,—and in calling you so, except those whom the most egregious envy prompts to speak the thing that is not, and the thing that they think not. And a great poet you unquestionably are; not near so great a poet as Milton or Spenser; but a much greater poet (and it is mere humbug to say you yourself don't think so) than Alexander Pope.[35] You see I don't make the least allusion to Shakespeare,[36] and I am sure, were you in my place, you would never dream of doing so any more than myself. It would be just as ridiculous to compare Milton to Shakespeare, as it would be to compare Pope to Shakespeare; and these the positive and the superlative being alike out of the question, what use would there be in lugging in you,—the comparative? Shakespeare stands by himself. He is not one of our race. You, Milton, and Pope, are all very clever men,—but there is not the least semblance of any thing superhuman about any one of you. But what, in the name of wonder, do you mean by this attempt of yours to persuade us that there is no difference of ranks among poets, except what depends on the difference of execution?[37] This is not the

[35] Pope was upheld poetically and morally by Byron in his *Letter on Pope*. "He is the moral poet of all civilization etc."—Byron, *Letters and Journals,* V, 560.

[36] In a note to the *Letter on Pope,* Byron wrote, "I shall not presume to say that Pope is as high a poet as Shakespeare and Milton."—*Ibid.*

[37] "There may or may not be, in fact, different 'orders' of poetry, but the poet is always ranked according to his execution, and not according to his branch of the art," wrote Byron in the *Letter*. And further, "The poet who *executes* best is the highest, whatever his department, and will ever be so rated in the world's esteem."—*Ibid.,* V, 553, 554.

point at all, my Lord, and you very well know it is not. The thing does not depend upon the nature of the execution, but on the order of the conceptions of the man. Shakespeare himself, in spite of all Schlegel's humbug, does not at all exceed all other men's excellence in the *execution* of his tragedies; and Martial does excel all other men in the *execution* of his epigrams. Tom Moore executes a song as well as Robert Burns—perhaps better, —but who, except a miss dying over her harpsichord, with an ensign at her back, ever dreamt of considering Tom Moore as great a poet as Burns. The "fact is," that Tom Moore, and Martial, and Pope, (I beg his pardon, however, for putting him alongside of Mr. Moore,) are not poets of the highest cast, because they have not conceptions of the highest cast,—and that Burns and Byron are, because they have. This, therefore, is a piece of utter humbug on your part; and I give you no credit for it, because it is a piece of humbug that every body will see through, just as well as myself. You might just as well have tried to persuade us that Gerard Douw was as great a painter as Titian or Salvator Rosa, because he painted Dutch doctors examining urinals better than either of them could have done. *"Est modus in rebus,"* my Lord; "there is reason in roasting of eggs;" and, even in humbugging, "SUNT CERTI DENIQUE FINES."[38] Could not you have uttered the plain truth about the Reverend Mr. Bowles?—viz. that *he* is no more a poet than he is the Emperor of China,—without plaguing the poor man with all that stuff about Pope, not one of whose satires Mr. Bowles ever did or ever can understand,—and whom Mr. Bowles had just as much right to edit as you, Lord Byron,

[38] Horace *Satires,* I: 1: 106.

would have to edit *Prideaux's Connections* [1716–18], or Jeremy Taylor's "Holy Living and Dying" [1650].

Mr. Bowles is no poet: in that, I take it, we are agreed. But he is a clergyman, and a most respectable clergyman, and so, in your letter to Mr. John Murray, you are pleased to say you consider him: and if so, permit me to ask you, what right had you to bring up against him an old story of a youthful prank, which is only so much the worse, because you have not told it at full length, and which, mark that, my Lord, you, according to your account, learned in the confidence of a private conversation?[39] You say that if Bowles had a right to allude to a scandalous story about Pope and Martha Blount, you also had a right to allude to a scandalous story about the Reverend Mr. Bowles, when he was a young man at college. It appears to me, that no one can be taken in by this piece of your Lordship's humbug, any more than by the specimen of it I have already commented on. Where did Mr. Bowles learn the story about Pope? In the MS. letters in the British Museum. Is this the same thing with hearing a story of a

39 In the *Letter* Byron does not tell the actual story but hints mysteriously: "If I were in the humor for story-telling, and relating little anecdotes, I could tell a much better story of Mr. B. than Cibber's [of Pope], upon much better authority, viz. that of Mr. B. himself. It was not related by *him* in my presence, but that of a third person, whom Mr. B. names oftener than once in the course of his replies."—Byron, *Letters and Journals,* V, 542. Moore told the story to Byron (*ibid.,* n. 1).

The Irishman points out, indeed, that both Bowles and Byron thought that *he* supported them:

". . . On the appearance of Lord Byron's answer to Mr. Bowles, I had the mortification of finding that, with a far less pardonable want of reserve, he had all but named me as his authority for an anecdote of his reverend opponent's early days, which I had, in the course of an after-dinner conversation, told him at Venice, and which,—pleasant in itself, and, whether true or false, harmless,—derived its sole sting from the manner in which the noble disputant triumphantly applied it."—*Ibid.,* V, 305 n.

living gentleman told by a friend of that gentleman over a bottle of claret? No, no; it is as different a thing as possible; and its effects are as different as possible, or, what is here the same thing, may be so. What harm can either Pope's feelings or Miss Blount's feelings receive from any story told about them a hundred years after they have been laid in their graves? Neither of them left any children,—even Mr. Bowles does not hint that they did,—therefore what is the harm that can possibly come to any one human being from the telling of the story? But how different is the case in regard to Mr. Bowles? He is alive,—though not merry,—preaching excellent sermons every Sunday, and printing abominable pamphlets every year. You know very well that neither I, nor any man of common judgment, could think the worse, either of Mr. Pope or Mr. Bowles, for a hundred such stories;—but do you think there are no respectable old and young ladies in Mr. Bowles's congregation, who may entertain, and who ought to entertain, very different views as to such matters, from such people as you and me? and can you really justify yourself to your own mind, when you think for a moment on the pain that idle and unwarrantable allusion of your's may have occasioned to these worthy people, and through them, and on their account, if not on his own, to this excellent divine? I cannot think of this part of your Lordship's conduct, without being quite shocked. I think it is even more abominable than your hits about poor Sam Coleridge's opium, and that for three sufficient reasons: First, because Coleridge won't care about your attacking his opium; whereas Mr. Bowles must and will care about your raking up his youthful levities: Secondly, because you might possibly have thought to do Coleridge good by making him diminish his dose;

whereas, according to your own statement,[40] Mr. Bowles has long since given up all frolics of the sort to which you allude: Thirdly, and lastly, and chiefly, because Coleridge is naturally as clever a man as your Lordship, and if he chose to give up his opium for a week, and to set about it in good earnest, (witness his "fire, sword, and famine,"[41]) could avenge himself abundantly, and give you, or any wicked wit in Europe, a thrashing to your heart's content; whereas, the worthy Mr. Bowles is a man quite unable to write any thing, that either your Lordship or any man alive could care a farthing for, and can do nothing but sit at home in his vicarage, moping and sighing, not even venturing to take his usual hand at whist with the good spinsters over the way, lest they should have heard of Lord Byron's "awful pamphlet," and

"Turn cold regards upon the reverend man."

"In fact" your conduct, in this particular, can only be explained in two ways, neither of them much to your honour. Either you have less imagination than I give you credit for, and (being, of course, quite incapable of having your own feelings wounded by any allusions or stories of this kind) do not imagine it possible that any other person can be differently constituted; that is to say, you can imagine a Corsair or a Juan, but you cannot imagine a timid, decent, worthy, stupid, pious clergyman of the Church of England; or you have more wickedness than

40 "But should I, for a youthful frolic, brand Mr. B. with a 'libertine sort of love,' or with 'licentiousness'? Is he the less now a pious or a good man, for not having always been a priest? No such thing; I am willing to believe him a good man, almost as good a man as Pope, but no better."—*Ibid.*, V, 542.

41 A reference to *Fire, Famine, and Slaughter. A War Eclogue* (1798), the scorching attack Coleridge directed at Pitt.

I suspected you of having, and knowing very well that such an allusion to such a story would give exquisite torture to Mr. Bowles, wrote and published the paragraph, for the express purpose of inflicting on him (who had done you no evil) that unjust and unnecessary pain. I am sorry for you if the first of these be the true explanation; doubly, trebly sorry, if the second be so. A man's eyes may become stronger than they have been: a man's imagination more extensive, but one might as well attempt to

> "Create a soul beneath the ribs of death,"[42]

as to give him a heart who, at your Lordship's time of life, has none. That is a lesson which no man can teach. For once believe what I say. I assure you this is not humbug.

After all, however, I spoke foolishly when I said there were but two possible keys to the mystery. There is a *third,* forgive me for not thinking of it sooner, which, if all some people say be true, may not improbably turn out to be the right one;—that is, the whole affair may be a fiction.[43] You may never have dined in company with any friend of Mr. Bowles's, in the way you describe; you may never have heard any scandalous story about Mr. Bowles from any man breathing; and you may have written the whole paragraph merely as a piece of humbug. I hope this is the true explanation; for humbug is indeed a pestilence very widely spread, and you are sadly infected with it,—but it is not an incurable disease; and I flatter

42 ". . . create a soul
Under the ribs of death."—Milton's *Comus,* lines 559–60.

43 In a letter to Murray, however, Byron repeated the tale, "*not* for the public." It was expunged by the editor.—Byron, *Letters and Journals,* V, 278.

myself, a little touch of my probe may not be the most unlikely thing in the world to give you, as well as some other of my patients, *"the turn,"* who shall, in due time, engage my affectionate attentions, for I cannot be administering to every body at the same moment.

But enough of Bowles. I say he is no poet, and you are a great poet; and I go on with the entity, leaving the nonentity to those who do love it. You are a great poet, but even with your poetry you mix too much of that at present very saleable article against which I am now bestirring myself. The whole of your misanthropy, for example, is humbug. You do not hate men, "no, nor woman neither,"[44] but you thought it would be a fine, interesting thing for a handsome young Lord to depict himself as a dark-souled, melancholy, morbid being, and you have done so, it must be admitted, with exceeding cleverness. In spite of all your pranks, (Beppo, &c. Don Juan included,) every boarding-school in the empire still contains many devout believers in the amazing misery of the black-haired, high-browed, blue-eyed, bare-throated, Lord Byron. How melancholy you look in the prints! Oh! yes, this is the true cast of face. Now, tell me, Mrs. Goddard, now tell me, Miss Price, now tell me, dear Harriet Smith, and dear, dear Mrs. Elton,[45] do tell me, is not this just the very look, that one would have fancied for Childe Harold? Oh! what eyes and eyebrows!—Oh! what a chin!—well, after all, who knows what may have happened. One can never know the truth of such stories. Perhaps her *Ladyship* was in the wrong after all.—I am sure if I had married such a man, I would have borne with all his little ec-

44 Shakespeare, *Hamlet,* II: 2: 302.

45 Miss Price is the heroine of Jane Austen's *Mansfield Park.* The other ladies are characters in her *Emma.*

centricities—a man so evidently unhappy.—Poor Lord Byron! who can say how much he may have been to be pitied? I am sure I would; I bear with all Mr. E.'s[46] eccentricities, and I am sure any woman of real sense would have done so to Lord Byron's: poor Lord Byron!—well, say what they will, I shall always pity him;—do you remember these dear lines of his—

"It is that settled ceaseless gloom,
The fabled Hebrew wanderer bore,
That will not look beyond the tomb,
But cannot hope for rest before."[47]

—Oh! beautiful! and how beautifully you repeat them! You always repeat Lord Byron's fine passages so beautifully. What think you of that other we were talking of on Saturday evening at Miss Bates's?[48]

——"Nay, smile not at my sullen brow,
Alas! I cannot smile again."[49]

I forget the rest;—but nobody has such a memory as Mrs. E. Don't you think Captain Brown[50] has a look of Lord Byron?

How you laugh in your sleeve when you imagine to yourself (which you have done any one half-hour these seven years) such beautiful scenes as these:—they are the triumphs of humbug: but you are not a Bowles: you ought to be (as you might well afford to be) ashamed of

[46] Mr. Elton is the vicar in *Emma*.

[47] "To Inez," lines 17–20, Byron's *Childe Harold,* Canto I, introduced between stanzas 84 and 85.

[48] Also from *Emma*.

[49] "To Inez," lines 1–2.

[50] Probably a child of Lockhart's brain, as are the eulogies bestowed on Byron.

them. You ought to put a stop to them, if you are able; and the only plan I can point out is, that of making a vow and sticking to it, as I have done, and ever, I hope, shall do, of never writing a line more except upon the anti-humbug principle. You say you admire Pope, and I believe you: well, in this respect, I should really be at a loss to suggest a better model; do you also, my Lord, "stoop to truth, and ⟨de⟩ moralize your song."[51] Stick to Don Juan: it is the only sincere thing you have ever written; and it will live many years after all your humbug Harolds have ceased to be, in your own words,

> "A school-*girl's* tale—the wonder of an hour."[52]

Perhaps you will stare at this last piece of my advice: but, nevertheless, upon my honour, it is as sincere as possible. I consider Don Juan as out of all sight the best of your works; it is by far the most spirited, the most straightforward, the most interesting, and the most poetical; and every body thinks as I do of it, although they have not the heart to say so. Old Gifford's[53] brow relaxed as he gloated over it; Mr. Croker[54] chuckled; Dr. Whitaker[55] smirked;

51 Pope, *Lines to Dr. Arbuthnot,* I, 347. The line is, "But stooped to truth and moralized his song."

52 The original of this quotation is "a schoolboy's tale"—Byron's *Childe Harold,* Canto II, stanza 2, line 6.

53 William Gifford (1756–1826) was at this time editor of Murray's *Quarterly Review*. Lockhart considered him and Jeffrey "men of great talent" but "very bad reviewers."—Lang, *Life of Lockhart,* I, 169.

54 See *Introduction,* section 3. John Wilson Croker (1790–1857) and Lockhart were intimates for many years, despite the fact that Croker did not favor Lockhart's appointment as editor of the *Quarterly Review* in 1825, and that Lockhart sometimes resented Croker's interference during his editorship.

55 Thomas Durham Whitaker (1750–1821), another contributor to the *Quarterly Review.*

Mr. Milman[56] sighed; Mr. Coleridge[57] (I mean not the madman, but the madman's idiot nephew) took it to his bed with him. The whole band of the Quarterly were delighted; each man in his own *penetralia,* (I except, indeed, Mr. Southey, who read the beginning very placidly, but threw the Don behind the fire when he came to the cut at himself, in the parody on the ten commandments[58]); but who should dare to say a word about such a thing in the Quarterly? Poor Mr. Shelley cannot publish a wicked poem which nobody ever read, or was likely to read, but the whole band were up in arms against him:[59] one throwing in his face his having set fire to a rotten tree when he was a boy at Eton; and another, turning over the leaves of his own travelling memorandum book to discover the very date at which Mr. Shelley wrote himself "Αθεος," in a Swiss album;[60] and the whole of these precious materials handed forthwith to——I know whom. But not so with the noble Don. Every body poring over the wicked, smiling face of Don Juan,—pi-

56 Henry Hart Milman (1791–1868) later became one of Lockhart's closest friends and was one of Lockhart's "most important allies on the *Quarterly*." In his *jeu d'esprit* on John Keats, Byron says the *Quarterly* killed the poet, and then

Who shot the arrow?
"The poet-priest Milman
(So ready to kill man)
Or Southey or Barrow."

57 John Taylor Coleridge (1790–1876) was at this time assistant editor of the *Quarterly*.

58 See n. 26 above.

59 An abusive review of Shelley's *Revolt of Islam* appeared in the *Quarterly* of April, 1819. See Introduction, section 2 b.

60 The traveler was Southey. Byron believed that Southey, through Coleridge, spread a gross libel in England about Shelley's personal life and his.—Byron, *Letters and Journals,* IV, 272. Very likely this fact explains Byron's rough treatment of Coleridge which Lockhart seemed at a loss to understand.

rated duo-decimo competing it all over the island with furtive quarto; but the devil a word of warning in the high-spirited, most ethical, most impartial Quarterly Review. No; never a word—because—because—the wicked book contained one line ending with

—"My grand-dad's narrative."[61]

—and its publisher was—no it was not—Mr. John Murray.

Firstly. They would not speak of it at all, because it would never have done to speak of it without abusing you; and that was the *"vetitum nefas,"* through which it is only real sons of the "Japeti genus"[62] (like me) that dare run. Secondly, They could not speak of it without praising it, and that would have been doing something against themselves—it would have amounted to little less than coming in as accessories to the crime of *lese majesté* against the liege Lord of the Quarterly Reviewers, and of all other reviewers who print their Reviews—Humbug. —But even this is nothing to the story that is told (God knows with what truth!) of Blackwood—I mean the *man* Blackwood, not the *thing* Blackwood,—the bibliopole, not the magazine. This worthy bibliopole, it is said, actually refused to have Don Juan seen in his shop;[63] *"pro-*

[61] Canto II, stanza 137. This work is by John Byron, Fourth Lord Byron (1723–1786), and is entitled *Narrative, containing an account of the great distresses suffered by himself and his companions on the coast of Patagonia* (S. Baker and G. Leigh, T. Davies, London, 1768).

[62] Horace *Carmina,* I: 3: 26–27: "Forbidden wrong"; "Iapetus' daring son" [Prometheus].

[63] William Blackwood (1776–1834) wrote to William Maginn on June 19, 1821: "As to your blarney of my being able to do this [i.e., write an article for *Maga* on *John Bull's Letter to Lord Byron*] myself, it is really too much for me to swallow. . . . Your idea as to how the thing should be done is admirable, and I wish to God you had time to fill up your sketch. I do most cordially agree with you that I deserve quizzing for refusing to

cul, procul, esto profane,"[64] was the language of the indignant Master William Blackwood to the intrusive Don Juan. Now, had Lord Byron, (forgive the supposition,) had Lord Byron sent Don Juan, with five hundred thousand million times more of the devil about him than he really has exhibited, to that well-known character Christopher North, Esq. with a request to have the Don inserted in his Magazine,—lives there that being with wit enough to keep him from putrefying, who doubts the great Kit would have smiled a sweet smile, and desired the right honourable guest to ascend into the most honourable place of his upper chamber of immortality? This is clear enough; and then came the redoubted Magazine itself,—(why, by the way, have you delayed so long publishing that letter upon it which many have seen, and of which all have heard?[65])—what could it do? could it refuse to

sell 'Don Juan,' and should not be spared in the article. The only apology I have to offer to *you* is this, that it proceeded partly from pique and partly from principle. When the book was published by Murray, I was just on the point of breaking with him. I had not had a letter from him for some months. He sent me copies of the book per mail, without either letter or invoice, so that when I received them I was not disposed to read it with a favourable eye. I did read it, and I declare solemnly to you, much as I admired the talent and genius displayed in it, I never in my life was so filled with utter disgust. It was not the grossness or blackguardism which struck me, but it was the vile, heartless, and cold-blooded way in which this fiend attempted to degrade every tender and sacred feeling of the human heart. I felt such a revolting at the whole book after I had finished it, that I was glad of the excuse I had, from Mr. Murray not writing me, for refusing to sell it. I was terribly laughed at by my friends here, and I daresay you will laugh as much still at my prudery and pique."—Mrs. Oliphant, *Annals of a Publishing House,* I, 380–81.

64 Virgil *Aeneid,* VI, 258: *"Procul o, procul este, profane!"* ("Keep aloof.")

65 In answer to "Remarks on Don Juan," *Blackwood's Magazine,* V, August, 1819, 512, Byron wrote *Observations upon an Article in Blackwood's Edinburgh Magazine,* which he alternately wished Murray to

row in the wake of the admiral? could the clay rebel against the potter? No, no; a set of obsequious moralists meet in a tavern,[66] and after being thoroughly maddened with tobacco smoke and whiskey punch, they cry out—"Well, then, so be it; have at Don Juan." Upon a table all round in a roar of blasphemy, and by men hot from ——'s,[67] and breathing nothing but pollution, furious paragraph after furious paragraph is written against a book of which the whole knot would have been happy to club their brains to write one stanza,—a book which they had all got by heart ere they set about reviewing it, and which thousands will get by heart after all the reviews they ever wrote shall have sunk into the "melodious wave"[68] of the same Lake, where now slumber gently side by side, the fallen and fettered angel of the "Isle of Palms"

---

publish and not to publish during 1820 and 1821. (I find fifteen references to the piece in volumes IV, V, and VI of Prothero's edition of Byron's *Letters.*) The piece, published posthumously, was at this time being circulated by Murray in manuscript form. Byron attributed the article in *Blackwood* to John Wilson, the famed "Christopher North."

66 Ambrose's, which within a year lent its name to *Blackwood's Noctes Ambrosianae.*

67 Lockhart probably means "Ambrose's," but in the review of John Bull's *Letter* in *Maga,* the word "Kirk" is supplied here! The portion of the *Letter* quoted in the review varies considerably from the present text: "A set of too rigid moralists meet in a tavern, and after being gently refreshed with tobacco smoke and whisky punch, they cry out—'Well, then, so be it; have at Don Juan.' Upon a table all round in a current of religious feeling, and by men hot from Kirk, and breathing nothing but piety, furious paragraph after furious paragraph is written against a book nearly as clever as if they had written it themselves."

The review continues with a statement that the drink was claret, not whisky punch, and that "it was on a Thursday evening, so that it could not be said that we were hot from Kirk."—*"Letter* [*By John Bull*] *to Byron," Blackwood's Magazine,* IX, July, 1821, 426.

68 *Childe Harold,* Canto I, stanza 62. Also Shelley's *Lines written among the Eugeanean Hills,* line 186.

[1812], and the thrice rueful ghost of the late "much and justly regretted" Dr. Peter Morris.[69]

From the pure "Quarterly," and its disowned, if not discarded, Cloaca,[70] the leap is not "Wilsonian" to the "Edinburgh."[71] Don Juan was not reviewed there neither; but Little's[72] poems were; "aye, there's the rub."[73] It was very right to rebuke Tom Moore for his filth; but what was his filth to the filth of Don Juan? Why, not much more than his poetry was (and is) to the poetry of Don Juan. This, indeed, was straining at the shrimp, and swallowing the lobster; and what was the reason for it? Your Lordship knows very well it is to be found in a certain wicked page of a certain wicked little book of yours called "English Bards and Scotch Reviewers" [1809],—the suppression of which, by the way, is another egregious piece of humbug on the part of your Lordship. Had you never written that little book, (I wish you would write a better on the same subject—now that you are a man)—Mr. Francis Jeffrey,[74] that grave doctor of morality, would

69 John Wilson wrote the *Isle of Palms*. "Morris" is Lockhart's pseudonym in *Peter's Letters to His Kinsfolk*.

70 Murray originally had an interest in *Maga,* but, shocked to the soul by its literary escapades and critical flagrancies, he withdrew his financial support in 1818. See William Blackwood's letter quoted in n. 63 above.

71 John Wilson was a Tory; the *Edinburgh Review* was radically Whig.

72 In 1801 Moore published *Poems by the Late Thomas Little.*

73 Shakespeare's *Hamlet,* III: 1: 65.

74 In *English Bards and Scotch Reviewers,* Byron liberally satirized the famous Jeffrey-Moore duel. Byron at this time took the scathing review of his *Hours of Idleness* to be Jeffrey's. It is now accepted as the work of Henry Brougham.

In reviewing Medwin's *Conversations of Lord Byron,* the *Blackwood* group indignantly rejected Medwin's statement that Byron was finally convinced of Brougham's authorship of the review that called forth *English Bards and Scotch Reviewers.*—"Lord Byron's Conversations," *Blackwood's Magazine,* XVI, November, 1824, 535. Evidently the *Blackwood* group hated to see their ancient enemy, Jeffrey, exonerated on any count.

have flourished his thong and laid on with all his might, and Don Juan would have scratched his back, for he would have thought a flea had skipped within his linens. The thong was not flourished, the healing stripe was withheld, and the Don slumbered undisturbed. The Review, however, has really ventured to allude to him since; yes, in an article on some verses of Mr. Procter,[75] commonly called *(Euphoniæ causâ)* by the romantic and soul-melting name of Barry Cornwall, among many other excellent things there is a timely and comfortable remark that the style of the said Mr. Procter does not bear so much resemblance to that of Don Juan as it does to that of Parisina [1816]. It would have been just as proper to inform the world that the parlour in which Mr. Procter writes (I have no doubt it is very neatly papered and contains some good *prints*) does not bear so much resemblance to Westminster Abbey as it does to the Parthenon of Athens: or that Mr. Procter himself, (if he were turned into stone and stuck up upon a pedestal) would bear more resemblance to the Antinous than to the Farnese Hercules; or that Mr. Francis Jeffrey, were he to go upon the stage, would do better in the part of Jack the Giant-killer than in that of the Giant.

Enough, however, for the present, of these gentlemen: for their hour is not yet come, and I meant no more than to give them a jog in passing. For the most part, I believe you were treated much in the same style by the other Reviewers. Many, indeed, took some notice of the Don: and among the rest "my grandmother" was not silent.[76] The good woman could have pardoned your obscenity. I have even my suspicions that she would have overlooked your

[75] "A Sicilian Story. With Diego de Montilla; and other poems, by Barry Cornwall," *Edinburgh Review,* XXXIII, January, 1820, 144–55.

blasphemy; but she could not away—no, not for her life—with your abominable insinuation, that you had tipped her a bribe. She could, in her own pure conscience, despise it, but she could not permit the thing to remain uncontradicted,[77] for fear of the effect it might produce on her "friends and the public." Now, the old dame's *friends,* if she had any, could not possibly know any thing of Don Juan; and the public had never heard of her till you mentioned her, which I must own you did in a somewhat unfilial fashion. For shame, young man; I wonder you were not afraid of a prosecution. What would you have said had my grandmother decked herself in her Sunday attire, and taken her staff in her hand (Shakespeare says, "there is no staff more reverend than one *tipped with horn*"[78]) and so gone up to the Mansion House[79] with the proper formal affidavit? What a condition would this have reduced you to? Could you ever have held up

[76] *The British Review,* edited by William Roberts (1767–1849) had attacked Byron. He retaliated in *Don Juan,* Canto I, stanzas 209–10:

> For fear some prudish readers should grow skittish,
> I've bribed my grandmother's review—the British.
>
> I sent it in a letter to the Editor,
> Who thank'd me duly by return of post—
> I'm for a handsome article his creditor;
> Yet, if my gentle Muse he please to roast;
> And break a promise after having made it her,
> Denying the receipt of what it cost,
> And smear his page with gall instead of honey,
> All I can say is—that he had the money.

[77] Roberts unwisely rebuked the author of *Don Juan* for the insinuation that he had accepted a bribe—*British Review,* XIV, August, 1819, 266–68. Byron, pleased that Roberts fell into the trap he had set, answered with the withering *"Letter to the Editor of 'My Grandmother's Review,'"* which was published in *The Liberal,* 1822.—Byron, *Letters and Journals,* IV, 346, 465.

[78] Shakespeare, *Much Ado About Nothing,* V: 4: 124.

[79] Official residence of the Lord Mayor of London.

your head after it? What would the world have said? I will tell you, if you can't guess. The world would have looked on smiling, and said, "Lord, what a pother! Cant *versus* Humbug! When will people learn sense enough to keep their differences to themselves?" But, in sadness, I think your behaviour, in this particular, was rather cruel. It is well known you broke my grandmother's old heart by your wicked joke. She never was herself again from that moment. She mumbled something about green fields, and chewed the sheet—and I felt her and she was cold—cold downwards[80]—and poor old granny gave up the ghost—and "dust to dust" was the word.

But now she is gone, I am not without hopes you may begin to remember her good advices, and perhaps, "take a thought and mend."[81] If Barry Cornwall were in your place, I am sure he would feel very tender-hearted. He would weep, as SPEED expresses himself, "like a young wench that has buried her grandam."[82]

I will not insult Don Juan by saying that his style is *not* like that of Signior Penseroso di Cornuaglia;[83] in truth, I think the great charm of its style is, that it is not much like the style of any other poem in the world. It is utter humbug to say, that it is borrowed from the style of the Italian weavers of merry *rima ottava;* their merriment is nothing, because they have nothing but their merriment; yours is every thing, because it is delightfully intermingled with and contrasted by all manner of serious things—murder and lust included. It is also mere *humbug* to accuse you of having plagiarized it from Mr. Frere's pretty

80 Parody of the description of Falstaff's death in Shakespeare's *King Henry V,* II: 3: 7–12. The *British Review* did collapse in 1822.

81 Robert Burns, *Address to the Deil,* line 22.

82 Shakespeare, *Two Gentlemen of Verona,* II: 1: 24.

83 Mr. Melancholy Cornwall.

and graceful little Whistlecrafts.[84] The measure to be sure is the same, but then the measure is as old as the hills. But the spirit of the two poets is as different as can be. Mr. Frere writes elegantly, playfully, very like a gentleman, and a scholar, and a respectable man, and his poems never sold, nor ever will sell. Your Don Juan again, is written strongly, lasciviously, fiercely, laughingly—every body sees in a moment, that nobody could have written it but a man of the first order both in genius and in dissipation;—a real master of all his tools—a profligate, pernicious, irresistible, charming Devil—and, accordingly, the Don sells, and will sell to the end of time, whether our good friend Mr. John Murray honours it with him *imprimatur* or doth not so honour it.[85] I will mention a book, however, from which I do think you have taken a great many hints—nay, a great many pretty full sketches for your Juan. It is one which (with a few more) one never sees mentioned in reviews, because it is a book written on the anti-humbug principle. It is—you know it excellently well—it is no other than FAUBLAS,[86] a book which con-

84 In 1818 John Hookham Frere (1769–1846) published four cantos of *Whistlecraft* (Prospectus and Specimen of an intended National Work by William and Robert Whistlecraft). Byron's *Beppo* was an imitation of this work.

85 Byron called Murray "the most timorous of all God's booksellers." *Don Juan* appeared without author's name or bookseller's. In a note appended to "Crabbe's Tales of the Hall," *Blackwood's Magazine,* V, August, 1819, 483, its publication was remarked upon: "We have just received a copy of *Don Juan,* (which we are happy to observe has not the respectable name of Lord Byron's Publisher on its Title-page). . . . It is indeed truly pitiable to think that one of the greatest Poets of the age should have written a Poem that no respectable Bookseller could have published without disgracing himself."

86 In *"Letter to Lord Byron," Blackwood's Magazine,* IX, July, 1821, 424, the reviewer of Lockhart's *Letter* said, "He [John Bull] has the face to praise the Chevalier de Faublas, a book which a gentleman would be ashamed to name." See Appendix B.

tains as much good fun as *Gil Blas,*[87] or *Moliere*[88]—as much good luscious description as the *Heloise;*[89] as much fancy and imagination as all the Comedies in the English language put together—and less humbug than any one given romance that has been written since Don Quixote—[90] a book which is to be found on the tables of Roués, and in the desks of divines and under the pillows of spinsters—a book, in a word, which is read universally—I wish I could add,—in the original. Your fine Spanish lady, with her black hair lying on the pillow, and the curly-headed little Juan couched under the coverlid,—she is taken—every inch of her—from the *Marquise de B*——; your Greek girl (sweet creature!) is *La petite Contesse,* but she is the better, because of her wanting even the semblance of being married. You have also taken some warm touches from Peregrine Proteus,[91] and if you read Peregrine over again you will find there is still more well worth the taking.

But all this has nothing to do with the charming *style* of Don Juan, which is entirely and inimitably your own—the sweet, fiery, rapid, easy—beautifully easy, anti-humbug style of Don Juan. Ten stanzas of it are worth all your Manfred [1817]—and yet your Manfred is a noble poem too in its way; and Meinherr von Goëthe[92] has exhibited no more palpable symptom of dotage than in his attempt

87 French novel in four parts (two in 1715, others in 1725 and 1735), by Alain René Lesage.

88 Molière's *Le Festin de Pierre* has Don Juan as its hero.

89 J. J. Rousseau, *Julie ou la Nouvelle Hèloïse* (1761).

90 In 1822 Lockhart, an ardent student of Spanish literature, published a new edition of *Don Quixote* (1605). Scott had begun the work, but because of Lockhart's superior fitness for the task, persuaded Lockhart to finish.—Lang, *Life of Lockhart,* I, 307.

91 Christoph Martin Wieland, *Geheime Geschichte des Philsophen Peregrinus Proteus* (1791). See Appendix B.

to persuade his *"lesende publicum"* that you stole it from his Faustus [1808–32];[93] for it is, as I have said, a noble and an original poem, and not in the least like either Don Juan or Faust, and quite inferior to both of them. I had really no idea what a very clever fellow you were till I read Don Juan. In my humble opinion, there is very little in the literature of the present day that will really stand the test of half a century, except the *Scotch* novels of Sir Walter Scott and Don Juan. *They* will do so because they are written with perfect facility and nature—because their materials are all drawn from nature—in other words, because they are neither made up of cant, like Wordsworth and Shelley, nor of humbug like Childe Harold [1812–18] and the City of the Plague [1816],[94] nor of Brunswick Mum, like the Rime of the Ancient Mariner [1798], nor of milk and water like Mr. Barry Cornwall.

The truth is, that the Baron and the Baronet stand quite by themselves: all the rest of the literati are little better than *canaille* compared to you. You are good friends, I am told, and I have no doubt you will continue so to the end of the chapter;—first, because you never can be rivals; and, secondly, because if you were rivals to-morrow, you are both men of the world and men of sense.

92 Lockhart may have visited Goethe in Germany in 1817. At his first meeting with Scott in 1818, Scott took Lockhart aside to talk of Goethe. —Lang, *Life of Lockhart,* I, 192.

93 Goethe wrote, "The tragedy of Manfred, by Lord Byron, is a most singular performance, and one which concerns me nearly. This wonderful and ingenious poet has taken possession of my *Faust,* and hypochondriacally drawn from it the most singular nutriment."—quoted in Lockhart's "The Faustus of Goethe," *Blackwood's Magazine,* VII, June, 1820, 239.

94 Byron, in his reference to *Marino Faliero,* lists Wilson's *City of the Plague,* among other works, as giving proof of the existence of "dramatic power somewhere."—Byron, *Poetry,* IV, 338–39.

Your ages are very different; yet, talking of you as authors go, you may both be said to be still young men. Some years ago there was a good deal of humbug about the Baronet's productions, and now I see scarcely a trace of it; and a few years hence, I don't know what should prevent you from exhibiting a reformation quite as complete. If you mean to do so, it must be by adhering to the key of Don Juan; and, if he means not to relapse, his plan is to stick to the key of Guy Mannering [1815]. Take my advice, both of you, and "know when you are well." Sir Walter has Scotland all to himself; and as for exhausting that or any other field of true nature—he and you are both quite aware that it is humbug to speak of it. War, love, life, death, mirth, sorrow, imagination, observation—who beyond the calibre of "my grandmother" ever thought or spoke of exhausting these things? And as for rivals in *his* field—who are they I pray you, or who are they ever likely to be? Mr. James Hogg, who represents haughty kings as stupid lairds, and lairds as drunken ploughmen, and ladies like haycock-wenches,—who turns Dundee into a highland sergeant—and highland sergeants into covenanters. No, no, Blackwood's Brownie[95] will never do, nor Mr. Allan Cunningham, whose mouth is so full of butter that it has no room for bread.[96] These are both of them clever fellows, indeed, and either of them worth all the Clares[97] that ever trod upon hobnails: but Scottish poetry numbers just three true geniuses, (and it is enough in all conscience,) and their names are Dun-

[95] Hogg's *Brownie of Bodsbeck* (1818) was published by Blackwood and Murray.

[96] Lockhart was really very fond of Hogg and Cunningham; to them he dedicated, in 1828, his *Life of Burns*.

[97] John Clare (1793–1864), a "Northamptonshire peasant," published in 1820 *Poems Descriptive of Rural Life and Scenery*.

bar, Burns, Scott,—and they are all of them enemies to humbug, at least I would have said so without hesitation, but for the sickening remembrance of the Ayrshire Ploughman's Sentimental Letters [published in 1802], which, upon my honour, I think are as nauseous as any thing even in Southey's Pilgrimage to Waterloo [1816], or your own imitations of Ossian,[98] or in Macpherson himself. As for "Marriage,"[99] that is indeed a much superior book to any that Hogg or Cunningham, or any of that sort will ever write—but then who does not remember the History of Triermaine?[100] Is Mr. Brougham the only person that is to be pardoned for confessing his "Marriage" a little too late?[101]—Scotland, therefore, is and will remain Sir Walter's. And what, you will say, is mine? I will tell you, Lord Byron: England is yours, if you choose to make it so.—I do not speak of the England of days past, or of the England of days to come, but of the England of the day that now is, with which, if you be not contented, you are about as difficult to please as a Buonaparte. There is nobody but yourself who has any chance of conveying to posterity a true idea of the *spirit* of England in the days of his Majesty George IV. Mr. Wordsworth may write fifty years about his "dalesmen;" if he paints them truly, it is very well; if untruly, it is no matter: but you know what neither Mr. Wordsworth nor any Cumberland stamp-master ever can know. You know the

98 Byron's *Hours of Idleness* contains some Ossianic imitations.

99 A novel by Susan Ferrier (1782–1854), published anonymously by Blackwood in 1818. Miss Ferrier was called Scott's "sister shadow."

100 Scott's *Bridal of Triermain* (1813) was passed off as William Erskine's work to bewilder Jeffrey.

101 Brougham's marriage on April 1, 1819, was kept secret for a month or two; and when Mrs. Brougham bore a seven-months' child, Brougham's Tory enemies had an even greater opportunity for malicious reference. See G. T. Garratt's *Lord Brougham* (London, Macmillan, 1935), 123.

society of England,—you know what English gentlemen are made of, and you very well know what English ladies are made of; and, I promise you, that *knowledge* is a much more precious thing, whatever you at present may think or say, than any *notion* you or any other Englishman ever can acquire either of Italians, or Spaniards, or Greeks. Do you really suppose, for a moment, (laying aside humbug) that you know any thing at all about either Venice or Ravenna worthy of being compared either as to extent or as to accuracy with what you know of London?—I mean of the true London, for as to the London east of Temple Bar, God knows there are enough of rhymsters, and prosers too, (whereof more anon,) who know, or ought to know, more about it than you ever can know, or ought to know; for no gentleman ought to know more of the polite Cockneys than may be learnt from reading one number of the Examiner,[102] nor more of the unpolite Cockneys than may be picked up from one evening of Mr. Mathews's "At Home."[103]

I believe the thing will bear looking into, that nothing worth much has ever been done either in literature, or in any of the sister arts, except by taking things as they are, or representing them as they are. Compare Homer's description of the old savage heroes with the descriptions of the same heroes even in Æschylus—far more with those in Sophocles, or Euripides, or Virgil, or any of all his imitators. Compare Tacitus, or Petronius, or Juvenal, with Seneca or Lucan. Compare Aristophanes with Xenophon.

102 Lockhart, in *Blackwood's Magazine,* coined the derisive term "Cockney School" for Leigh Hunt's circle and *The Examiner.*

103 Charles Matthews (1776–1835), an English comedian, appeared from 1808–24 in a series of original sketches called "At Homes." Lockhart met Matthews in Edinburgh.—Lang, *Life of Lockhart,* I, 294. Byron liked Matthews.

Compare Lucian, or Swift, or Montaigne, or Le Sage, or Cervantes, with any of their contemporaries—except the last of them, by the way, for he was the contemporary of Shakespeare, and died (odd enough!) on the same day with him, and I doubt if two such fine fellows ever died on the same day before or since. Compare Boccaccio's novels with Petrarch's sonnets. Compare Goëthe's life of himself with his Sorrows of Werther. Compare Horace with Ovid, or with any body but Pope. Compare Hogarth with Sir Joshua, or Wilkie[104] with Fuseli, or Baillie Jarvie[105] with the goblin-groom, or Flittertigibbet,[106] or Mrs. Mucklebacket, junior, with Mrs. Mucklebacket, senior,[107] —or Lord Byron in the letter on the Reverend William Lisle Bowles with Lord Byron on the field of Talavera,[108] (where your English heart burned within you, although you had humbug enough to deny it.) Compare Lord Byron when he is describing a beautiful woman, or when he is quizzing Southey or Sotheby[109] with Lord Byron when he is puffing old Samuel Rogers, the banker, and pretending (what vile humbug!) to class him among the great poets of England, who has only written a very, very few lukewarm verses in his day;[110] albeit it may be most

104 Lockhart did not admire Sir David Wilkie's painting of Scott and his family.—*Ibid.*, II, 272.

105 Character in Scott's *Rob Roy*.

106 "Flibbertigibbet" appears in *King Lear* (III:4) and in Scott's *Kenilworth* (January, 1821).

107 Characters in Scott's *The Antiquary*.

108 *Childe Harold,* Canto I, stanzas, 40–42.

109 In *Beppo,* stanza 73, line 1, William Sotheby is Botherby, the "solemn, antique gentleman of rhyme."

110 In the *Letter on Pope,* Byron writes, "I had the honour of meeting Mr. Bowles in the home of our venerable host," Rogers, "the last Argonaut of classic English poetry, and the Nestor of our inferior race of living poets."—Byron, *Letters and Journals,* V, 537.

This "puff," however, evidently did not please Rogers, for Byron writes

true that he hath given a great many piping hot dinners —or still worse, perhaps, with the same Lord Byron, when he is writing down Wordsworth an ass, who, (with all his foibles,) he well knows, has put more genius (now and then) into ten lines, than all the poetical bankers in Christendom will ever be able to comprehend—and this for no earthly reason, except that he, (Lord Byron,) and the stamp-master did not take kindly to each other when they met, and that he, (Lord Byron,) knows the stamp-master is wrapped round in vanity, fold above fold, like one of Belzoni's[111] mummies, and that the least touch of sarcasm from one who really can be sarcastic, will probably put the stamp-master's swaddling-bands into such a flutter, that he, the stamp-master, shan't be able to compose himself for a single "Mood of my mind" during the rest of the season. Wherever you find them in short, compare reality with vision, sincerity with insincerity, honesty with humbug,—and there you will see what I mean when I advise you to continue the Don—on, through all his cantos, (observe I don't mean to continue it as wickedly as it is begun, but as sincerely)—to bring the Don forthwith into England—to put him to school at Harrow, and to college at Cambridge,—to lodge him at the Clarendon, and make him see the world,—as you yourself have seen it,—and de-

---

John Murray: "I hear that Rogers is not pleased with being called 'venerable'—a pretty fellow: if I had thought that he would have been so absurd, I should have spoken of him as defunct—as he really is."—*Ibid.*, V, 270.

111 Lockhart, who met Giovanni Battista Belzoni at Oxford in 1812, years before the famous discoveries in Egypt, did not find him amusing.—Lang, *Life of Lockhart,* I, 56.

Byron wrote in 1821 regarding Belzoni's account of his discoveries, "Belzoni is a grand traveller, and his English is very prettily broken."—Byron, *Letters and Journals,* V, 245.

scribe it as Sir Walter Scott has described Captain Clutterbuck.[112]

I know very well what a great many very knowing people, very shrewd people, very superior, very deep-thinking "earnest" people will say, when they read what I have just written. They will say, "Here now is a fellow that thinks himself a judge of literature, and yet, it is evident, he has only an eye and a relish for one particular species of literary excellence. He enjoys what is coarse, comic, obvious to every capacity,—but he has neither heart nor soul for the grand, the sublime, the pathetic, the truly *imaginative.*" You will say no such thing: you have discovered, many pages ago, that I am *up to trap* [i.e., "cunning" or "knowing"]: and you know quite well that nobody *can* enjoy in a rational manner any one species of literary excellence, without being able to enjoy many kinds of it. But fine words are the very essence of humbug; and men-tailors and women-tailors are made to be taken in by them. None of these worthy people have ever read Longinus, but you and I have;[113] and we know full well that what he considers as the true point of ambition in writing, his famous "ὕψος"[114] has nothing whatever to do with what "the fine spirits of the earth" talk about under the fine names of "the sublime," and so forth. The sublime of Longinus means nothing whatever but the *"energetic."* Does any man, not an *illustrissimus,* imagine that Longinus would ever have quoted Sappho's very strongly and voluptuously written love-song as a speci-

112 The feigned editor of some of Scott's works.

113 In *Don Juan,* Canto I, stanza 204, Byron says he will call his poetical commandments:

> Longinus o'er a Bottle,
> Or, Every Poet his *own* Aristotle.

114 Sublimity.

men of what the Alisons[115] call the sublime? There is not a single shred of the true sublime either in Southey, or his imitator Milman, or in Mrs. Radcliffe, or her very poor imitator Maturin.[116] There is a great deal of it in the life of Benvenuto Cellini. There is sublimity in Burke's political pamphlets, but not a whit in his Essay on the Sublime [1756]. Wherever energetic thoughts are expressed in energetic language, there I see the sublime: and there I am sure you see it. Mr. Wordsworth, no doubt, thinks the Excursion is very sublime. Now, I could point out about half a dozen pages in it that are so, and about two hundred pages that are no more sublime than so many bedaubed paper-kites, flying over the steeple (if steeple there be) of Grassmere church. The most sublime things in all Mr. Wordsworth's writings are, perhaps, those passages in prose, (I mean in prose which he himself acknowledges to be prose,)[117] in which he acknowledges his feelings of wrath and scorn for the Reviewers; and, by the way, I did great injustice to the Laureate, when I charged him with the want of sublimity. His vanity is at all times quite sublime, and the best proof of this is, that it makes every one split their sides with laughing. What can be more sublime than his *"exegi monumentum"*[118] at the close of all his great, lumbering, unreadable botheration about Brazil?[119] What, under heaven, is more sub-

115 Archibald Alison, *Essay on Nature and Principles of Taste* (1790).

116 Charles Robert Maturin (1764–1823) was praised and encouraged by Scott and Byron to produce his tragedy *Bertram,* in which Kean appeared in 1816.

117 Byron wrote in *English Bards and Scotch Reviewers,* lines 241–42, that Wordsworth

> . . . both by precept and example shows
> That prose is verse, and verse is merely prose.

118 "I have completed a monument."—Horace *Odes,* III: 30: 1.

lime than his grave, serious, downright panegyric upon himself for his "*introduction*" (as he complacently enough calls it) of hexameter verse into English literature?[120]

——"I first adventure; follow me who list."[121]

I myself intend to follow him: I intend to tip him a score or two of as good hexameters as ever he filled with the blended sublimities of vanity and blasphemy ere I have done with him. They will say, here's a man talking of vanity, and calling his own pamphlets sublime in the same breath. (By *they,* in that sentence, I mean what Southey calls "the Duncery,"[122] a numerous and very fine body of men, among whom Southey himself sometimes serves as a volunteer, and in which, moreover, he greatly distinguishes—at all the costs usual with volunteers.) But I don't mind all this—no, not the balancing of a single

[119] "Timothy Tickler," in the *Noctes Ambrosianae,* No. VI, speaks of the conclusion of Southey's "Brazil Balaam," i.e., *History of Brazil,* 1810–19: "Thus saith the Doctor—'Thus have I finished one of those great and lasting works, to which, in the full vigour of manhood, I looked forward as the objects of a life of literature.'—'Tis something like that, however—did you ever hear such like stuff?"

Odoherty answers, "Often from the Lakers. They're a high speaking set of boys."—*Blackwood's Magazine,* XII, December, 1822, 698.

[120] In his preface to *A Vision of Judgment,* Southey wrote: "Having long been of opinion that an English metre might be constructed in imitation of the ancient hexameter, which would be perfectly consistent with the character of our language, and capable of great richness, variety, and strength, I have now made the experiment."—Southey, *Poetical Works,* X, 195.

[121] Southey thought blank verse the greatest meter. "But I am satisfied also that the English hexameter is a legitimate and good measure, with which our literature ought to be enriched; 'I first adventure; follow me who list!' "—*Ibid.*, X, 202. (The quotation comes from the prologue to Joseph Hall's *Virgidimiarum, Sixe Books. First three Bookes of Toothless Satyrs* (London, Thomas Creede, 1597). The next line is, "And be the second English satirist.")

[122] A name bestowed on reviewers in the preface to *A Vision of Judgment.*—Southey, *Poetical Works,* X, 199.

spondee.[123] My pamphlet speaks the truth, and therefore my pamphlet *is* sublime; just as Mr. Southey rises to the sublime, when he says plump out, in plain English, that he thinks himself the greatest genius that has arisen in Europe these two thousand years,—an opinion, indeed, which would be quite just, were Mr. Southey what he considers himself; for it is quite evident that he thinks himself Milton, and Thucidides, and Clarendon, and Dryden, and Jeffrey, and Plato, and Tom Moore, and Burke, all in one. Were that the case, Mr. Southey himself would be sublime; at present, I see little sublimity about him, except what lies in the energetic, magnanimous, heroic, magnificence of his vanity. Horace said of himself he had erected a monument *"ære perennius:"*[124] the Laureate has at least the credit of having reared one of the genuine metal itself. Heavens! what a rumpus! why does not the King knight the Laureate?

But all this is mere parenthesis. I had a great many things to say to you, and I must not be kept from saying them by Mr. Southey. One of the things I was most anxious to say was, that I wished very much (after you have finished Don Juan) you would really in good earnest turn your mind to the drama. I don't think much of your Faliero [1820].[125] It is a failure. But your other works convince me that you might write both tragedies and comedies of the very highest merit, if you chose. You ought to choose it; because you may depend upon it these are, after

123 Southey wrote that the English language has "not a single instance of a genuine native spondee."—*Ibid.*, X, 198.

124 "More lasting than brass."—Horace *Odes*, III: 30: 1.

125 Byron objected strenuously to having a version of *Marino Faliero* presented on the stage. It was, however, brought out, and was a complete failure. Of the affair Byron wrote, "It seems a sort of dramatic Calvinism—predestined damnation, without a sinner's own fault."—Byron, *Letters and Journals*, V, 286.

all, the true *forms* for a man that understands human nature on both sides as you do, and is able, as you are, to express in capital English whatever you do understand. You should undoubtedly become a great dramatist, and so should Sir Walter, and I think, whatever you say, you must both have a strong hankering after the stage; although either of you, as the stage now stands, would have done very foolishly to begin the career with the stage. I say it would have been a very foolish thing to do so; and one excellent reason for what I say is, that there is no money (worth speaking of) to be had at present by writing for the stage. Now, Sir Walter has made a fortune by his books, and you will do so in good season too; and nothing can be more proper, because, if you did not, your booksellers would sell your books just as dear as they do, and pocket double as much as they do; whereas, all the world knows they have pocketed, and are pocketing, by both of you, quite as much as is at all good for them.

Before you begin, therefore, you and the Baronet should lay your heads together to have the law of dramatic literary property altered, which there is no question could easily be accomplished between you: for every body likes and admires Sir Walter, and every body dreads and admires you; and nobody in parliament would venture to oppose a scheme, which should be known to have originated with "the illustrious twain." You should lay your heads together on this matter, "like two girls both sewing of one flower upon one sampler,"[126] and I am sure Can-

[126] An allusion to a passage in Shakespeare, *A Midsummer Night's Dream,* III: 2: 210–15.

[127] George Canning (1770–1827). Lockhart met Canning in London in 1824 and was assured by William Wright that Canning approved his being appointed editor of the *Quarterly Review.*—Lang, *Life of Lockhart,* I, 346, 366.

ning[127] and Plunkett,[128] and Peel,[129] and the Speaker,[130] and Dicky Martin,[131] (the only men of letters in the House of Commons,) and Grenville,[132] and Holland,[133] and Wellesley,[134] (the only men of letters in the House of Lords,) would lend you all the assistance in their power. If the law of dramatic property were put on a proper footing, you and Sir Walter would write English and Scotch tragedies and comedies—and Theodore Hook[135] and I would take pains upon our farces—and then who should dare to speak of the theatre being an unfashionable place? Theatres would not be made to yield to routs and conversaziones *then,* because all the world knows that both finery and flirtation can be displayed to as much advantage in a well-cushioned box as any where else; and Lady Castlereagh,[136] and Lady Salisbury,[137] and Lady Staf-

128 William Conyngham Plunkett, first Baron Plunkett (1764–1854).

129 Sir Robert Peel (1788–1850), who attended Harrow with Byron.

130 Charles Manners-Sutton, Viscount Canterbury (1780–1845), was speaker from 1817–35.

131 Richard Martin (1754–1834) was called by George IV "Humanity Martin." He was one of the founders of the Society for the Prevention of Cruelty to Animals.

132 William Wyndham Grenville, Baron Grenville (1759–1834).

133 Henry Richard Vassall Fox, Lord Holland (1770–1840), created at Holland House a center for Whig literary and political movements. Byron was a frequent visitor there during the days he was London's social lion.

134 Richard Colley Wellesley, Marquis Wellesley (1760–1824).

135 Lockhart met Theodore Hook (1788–1841) a dramatist and satirist, in London in 1824. Scott hated "funny, easy companions" like Hook and Maginn. Lockhart wrote his *Life of Hook* in 1843.—Lang, *Life of Lockhart,* I, 346, 373; II, 265.

136 Emily Ann, daughter of John Hobart, second earl of Buckinghamshire, wife of Viscount Castlereagh, leader of the House of Commons.

137 Frances Mary Gascoyne, wife of the second Marquis of Salisbury. Lockhart met Lady Salisbury in 1832 and thereafter was a frequent visitor at Hatfield House. Lang, *Life of Lockhart,* II, 28.

ford,[138] and so forth, would go into the thing with a good grace, and the Countess San Antonio, and Mrs. Thompson,[139] and all the so-so set, would be fain to follow their example, if once it were given; and the second Mrs. Wood would be as sure a card as the first Mrs. Wood, and all the citizens, "after their kind,"[140] would be forthcoming on the evening of the third day of the dramatic re-creation,—and the King (God bless him!) would not go once in the twelvemonth, with all his stars and trumpets, as if Seringapatam were to be taken—and nobody would stay away but Haynes,[141] and Knowles,[142] and Barry Cornwall, "as melancholy as a gib cat;"[143]—and well he might, because such things as "the Mirandola"[144] (for every thing is *the* with the Cockneys and the Lakers) would have no more chance of being red-lettered into notoriety in those days, than they have of being red-lettered into fame now. It absolutely makes one sick to think of the English stage that used to be such a fine masculine place, and of its being reduced to the exhibition of such smooth-chinned heroes as these cockney Italians!—and the worst of it is,

138 Lockhart dined with Lord Stafford frequently after 1825.—*Ibid.*, II, 77.

139 Probably social figures of the day, as are the first and second Mrs. Wood mentioned below. A Countess St. Antonio is mentioned by Earl Grey in a letter to Mr. Creevy, dated December 15, 1827.—Thomas Creevy, *The Creevy Papers, A Selection from the Correspondence and Diaries of the late T. Creevy*, ed. by Sir Herbert Maxwell (New York, Dutton and Company, 1904), 483.

140 Genesis 1: 21.

141 John Thomson Haynes (1799–1843) wrote melodramas of the blood and thunder type.

142 James Sheridan Knowles (1784–1862).

143 Shakespeare, *Henry IV*, Part I, I: 2: 83.

144 William Charles Macready (1793–1873) appeared in Knowles's *Virginius* as Virginius in 1820. In 1821 he played Mirandola in Cornwall's *Mirandola*. These characters were the "cockney Italians."

that the actors have really so much merit, that they almost *can* make even such creatures as these appear tolerable; the more is the shame or the pity that they are willing or obliged to take trouble about them. Macready[145] now, for example, is neither a Kemble[146] nor a Kean,[147] but he is a clever spirited fellow, with thews and sinews to his legs, and I don't know any good reason why he should be seen strutting up and down, torturing soul and twisting body, to make something out of nothing, when we have three or four good tragedians already IN ACTU, as the schoolmen say, and at least two more *in potentia,* meaning Sir Walter and yourself.

This, I assure you, will be much better than writing certain letters, which, although you say they "never can be published," most undoubtedly will, one day or other, be published, and have been written, one and all of them, for the express purpose of being published,—and which, if all tales be true, will do no great good when they are published, either to your reputation, if you be alive, or to the feelings of your friends, if you be dead. And, since I have mentioned your friends, I shall also take the liberty to say, that I think this would be much more creditable than abusing some of them,—your wife, for example, in the manner in which you have been doing. For myself, God knows, I am one of the last people in the world that would wish to set the example of interfering improperly

145 See n. 144 above. Macready called Lockhart "that reptile of criticism."

146 John Philip Kemble (1757–1823) was considered by Byron "the most super-natural of actors."

147 Edmund Kean (1787–1833) was seen by Lockhart in Edinburgh in 1816. Lockhart particularly admired his Othello.—Lang, *Life of Lockhart,* I, 111. Comparing Kean and Kemble, Byron wrote, "Kemble's Hamlet is perfect;—but Hamlet is not Nature. Richard is a man; and Kean is Richard."—Byron, *Letters and Journals,* II, 386.

in the private, and more particularly in the domestic affairs of any man. But, if I were to permit myself to hazard an opinion on a matter, with which, I confess, I have so very little to do, I should certainly say that I think it quite possible you were in the right in the quarrel with Lady Byron,[148]—nay, that I think the odds are very decidedly in favour of your having been so; and that was the opinion, I remember it very well, of by far the *shrewdest* person of my acquaintance, (I need not say woman,) at the time when the story happened. But this is nothing. The world had nothing whatever to do with a quarrel between you and Lady Byron, and you were the last man that should have set about persuading the world that the world had or could have any thing to do with such a quarrel. What does a respectable English nobleman or gentleman commonly do, when his wife and he become so disagreeable to each other, that they must separate? Why did you not ask of yourself that plain question, the morning you found you and Lady Byron could not get on together any longer? I wish you had done so, and acted upon it, from my soul: for I think the whole of what you did on that unhappy occasion, was in the very worst possible taste, and that it is a great shame you have never been told so in print—I mean in a plain, sensible, anti-humbug manner, from that day to this. What did the world care whether you quarrelled with your wife or not? At least, what business had you to suppose that the world cared a single farthing about any such affair? It is surely a very good thing to be a clever poet; but it is a much more essential thing to be a gentleman; and why, then, did you,

148 "She should have married Wordsworth," Henley once remarked; "he would have had plenty of opportunity to learn 'how awful goodness is.' "—quoted by Chew, *Byron in England,* 21.

who are both a gentleman and a nobleman, act upon this the most delicate occasion, in all probability, your life was ever to present, as if you had been neither a nobleman nor a gentleman, but some mere overweeningly conceited poet? To quarrel with your wife over night, and communicate all your quarrel to the public the next morning, in a sentimental copy of verses![149] To affect utter broken-heartedness, and yet be snatching the happy occasion to make another good bargain with Mr. John Murray! To solicit the compassion of your private friends for a most lugubrious calamity, and to solicit the consolation of the public, in the shape of five shillings sterling per *head,*—or perhaps, I should rather say, per *bottom!* To pretend dismay and despair, and get up *for the nonce* a dear pamphlet!—O, my Lord, I have heard of mean fellows making money of their wives, (more particularly in the army of a certain noble duke,[150]) but I never heard even of a commissary seeking to make money of his wife in a meaner manner than this of yours! and then consider, for a moment, what beastliness it was of you to introduce her Ladyship in Don Juan,[151]—indeed, if I be not much mistaken, you have said things in that part of the poem, for which, were I her brother, I should be very well entitled to pull your nose,—which (don't alarm yourself) I have not, at present, the smallest inclination or intention to do.

149 Byron had fifty copies of *Fare Thee Well* and *A Sketch* printed in pamphlet form by Murray to be distributed among his private friends. A pirated edition was soon brought forth, however, and the poems were reprinted in the newspapers.—Byron, *Poetry,* III, 531–32.

150 In 1809, the Duke of York, commander-in-chief of the army, was accused of having made wrong use of military patronage. His mistress, Mary Ann Clarke, undoubtedly received money from army officers by promising to use her influence with the Duke. The cause against the Duke was not proved, but the scandal created a public furor.

151 "Donna Inez" in *Don Juan* is Lady Byron.

—Just suppose, for a moment, that any other peer of the realm (bar Irish) had behaved himself as you have done, and I fear are still doing, what a letter you would have written about him! Would even Billy Bowles have had reason to envy such a person!

This is a part of your humbug, however, on the success of which I can by no means congratulate you. Your verses read very well the day they were published; but people soon began to reflect, that when a man is really afflicted by a domestic calamity, it is by no means natural for him to make the public his confidant. Nobody believed but that (for all your Werterian lamentations over the loss of your domestic happiness) you might have made up the quarrel had you chose; for nobody doubts that a very extraordinary man must have extraordinary power, if he pleases, over a very ordinary woman. Every body whispered "humbug," when you talked about your heart being broken, just as they did when you talked about the extreme ugliness of the poor governess,[152]—whom nobody had ever pretended to think ugly, and whom I, for one, and your Lordship for another, always thought *(sub rosâ)* a very comely and kissable sort of person,—or, as they did when you published that very pathetic stanza of your's, beginning,

"Ada! sole daughter of my house and heart."[153]

The object of that stanza was, of course, to humbug women and children into an idea that you were very much distressed with being separated from the sweet little *Ada!*—But *men* knew, even then, that you might have rocked her cradle to pieces had you had a mind,—and we

[152] A Mrs. Clermont. Byron attacked her in *A Sketch*.
[153] *Childe Harold,* Canto III, stanza 1.

all know now that you have been enjoying yourself very heartily for four or five years among ladies and misses of quite another kind, without ever disturbing either your dinner or your nap, by any thoughts either about the Right Hon. Lady Byron, or the now (I am happy to inform you) very healthy, plump, and chubby-cheeked Hon. Miss Ada Byron. This is a long letter, but when one writes to a friend abroad, a short one is mere humbug.

Your's,

JOHN BULL.

Printed by William Wright, Fleet-Street.

APPENDICES

APPENDIX A

Byron in Blackwood's Magazine

THE treatment of Byron in *Blackwood's Magazine* in the years between 1817 and 1825 is inconsistent and contradictory; yet the mud and incense curiously intermingled in the references to "the noble Exile" are hardly more breath-taking than the alternate caressing or evisceration of Wordsworth and other contemporaries in the same periodical. By judicious quotation from *Maga,* one may, indeed, damn or apotheosize any contemporary writer. After Byron's death, *Blackwood's Magazine* settled down at last to a fairly even course in Byronic criticism, admitting the poet's faults but admiring his genius and defending his memory. In this study, the year 1825 has been chosen as the limit for Byron's treatment in *Maga* because at the end of that year Lockhart migrated to London to assume the editorship of the *Quarterly Review.* After his marriage in 1823 William Maginn had migrated to London also, to employ his inexhaustible pen in the journals and periodicals of the metropolis. Owing more and more to John Wilson in the years that followed, *Maga* in 1826 entered into its maturity. From *Blackwood's Contributors' Book, 1826–1846,* now in the National Library of Scotland, the authorship of articles after 1825 in *Blackwood's Magazine* may usually be established.

The articles listed in the pages that follow offer a review of Byron's work and afford particularly a sort of seismic chart of contemporary horror at, but grudging admiration of, the first eleven cantos of *Don Juan*. The bitter attack on the first two cantos of the poem, by John Wilson or Lockhart, in August, 1819, is answered by "Metrodorus" in the magazine of December, 1819, just as Cantos III, IV, and V are defended by "Harry Franklin" in August, 1821. Surely Maginn's brilliant fourth *Noctes* of July, 1822, in which "Odoherty" and Byron himself are the speakers, more than atones for any incidental slurs at the poet elsewhere in *Maga*. What can be more superlative praise than "Odoherty's" exclamation, "I had rather have written a page of Juan than a ton of Childe Harold!" Again, the most violent of all the attacks, by Maginn and Lockhart, on Cantos VI, VII, and VIII of *Don Juan,* in July, 1823, is more than counterbalanced by Lockhart's splendid praise of Cantos IX, X, and XI, in September of the same year—praise that William Blackwood feared (in a letter to Wilson) might be "apt to startle weak minds." All the more extraordinary is *Maga's* treatment of Byron's masterpiece because the *Blackwood* group was particularly hostile to the poet in 1822 and 1823 on account of his association with the "Cockney" Leigh Hunt in the publication of *The Liberal* in Italy. Altogether, *Maga* took a leading part among periodical publications in recognizing *Don Juan* as a work destined to rank high in English literature; and altogether, *Maga* praised Byron superlatively as "this great and godlike poet of England."

The ascriptions in the following outlines up to 1826 are not altogether satisfactory. Sometimes a reference in a letter included by Mrs. Gordon or Mrs. Oliphant clinches authorship definitely. More often the authorities cited appear to have arrived at their ascriptions by guesswork—or, what is not at all the same thing, appear to have quoted earlier authorities who arrived at their ascriptions by guesswork. I am fortunate in having the attributions to Maginn from Professor Ralph M. Wardle, of the University of Omaha, a leading authority on Maginn in this country. His attributions, like the attributions to Lockhart of Miss M. Clive Hildyard, have usually some specific source and may therefore be considered conclusive. Rarely, the style of an article has made me assign the piece to John Wilson or another. But a question mark after an author's name means little more than that the article in question *may* have been written by him.

1. *The more important Criticisms and passing Allusions*

"Manfred"

June, 1817. I, 289–95 Wilson[1]

"To no poet was there ever given so awful a revelation of the passions of the human soul." Byron's soul has now become imbued with nature,—and in the third canto of *Childe Harold* he "came into competition with Wordsworth upon his own ground, and with his own weapons; and in the first encounter he vanquished and overthrew him. His description of the stormy night among the Alps . . . is alone worth all the dull metaphysics of the Excursion."

The present "very singular, and, we suspect, very imperfect poem" has the same scene as *Childe Harold,* Canto III,

[1] Byron wrote Murray, October 12, 1817: "The review in the Magazine you say was written by Wilson? it had all the air of being a poet's, and was a very good one."—Byron, *Letters and Journals,* IV, 175 and n. Compare, also, Chew, *Byron in England,* 113, and *Memoirs and Correspondence of Coventry Patmore,* ed. by Basil Champneys (London, Bell, 1900, 2 vols.), II, 433; hereafter referred to as *Patmore.*

but it deals with the world of spirits; though every page of *Manfred* teems with imagery and passion, its author's mind is so often overborne by the strength and novelty of its descriptions, that "the composition as a whole, is liable to many and fatal objections." Finally, Byron has a very imperfect knowledge of blank verse, which though flowing, vigorous, and sonorous, is too often in this poem slovenly and careless to a great degree.

"The Lament of Tasso"
November, 1817. II, 142–44 Wilson[2]

Byron's heroes are "a noble band of Brothers . . . whose looks, thoughts, words, and deeds had troubled us by their wild and perturbed grandeur." In "The Lament of Tasso," however, Byron has "allowed his soul to sink down into gentler and more ordinary feelings." This poem "possesses much of the tenderness and pathos of the Prisoner of Chillon." Its author has used an effective restraint in his picturing of the sorrowing of Tasso.

Fourth Canto of *Childe Harold*
May, 1818. III, 216–18* Wilson[3]

Byron's "everlasting self-representation or self-reference" in his poetry, instead of being the essential fault of it, is that

[2] Mrs. Mary Gordon, *Christopher North: A Memoir of John Wilson*, ed. by R. Shelton Mackenzie (New York, W. J. Widdleton, 1866), 187; hereafter referred to as *Christopher North;* Mrs. Oliphant, *Annals of a Publishing House,* I, 262, 264. One of the "Notices to Correspondents" of *Maga* of August, 1817, promises the article for the next number; but a "Notice from the Editor" of October explains that the piece has been "necessarily delayed."

*The pagination in *Blackwood's Magazine* frequently goes wrong. Thus this article runs from pp. 216–224, which is followed by pp. 217 and 218. Wherever a similar situation occurs, the page number is followed by *.

[3] Mrs. Gordon, *Christopher North,* 187. Wilson also wrote a brilliant review of the fourth canto of *Childe Harold* for the *Edinburgh Review* of August, 1818.—*Ibid.,* 157. See also Smiles, *A Publisher and His Friends,* I, 398, 400.

that "constitutes its real excellence, and gives it power, sovereign and despotical." Though his heroes are himself, his unequalled intenseness of passion precludes any complaint of repetition. . . . "It is cold and unmeaning to say, that in the third canto of Childe Harold, he imitated or competed with the author of the Excursion. He followed him—he was led by him—to the same eternal fountain of all beauty and all grandeur. . . ." Wilson pronounces the fourth canto of *Childe Harold* "the finest, beyond all comparison, of Byron's poems."

"Letter tô the Author of Beppo"
June, 1818. III, 323–29

"Presbyter Anglicanus" solemnly warns Byron that although other great poets have dealt with wickedness, their purpose was to improve mankind, not to debase. "Your predecessors, in one word, my Lord, have been the friends—you are the enemy of your species." Byron has destroyed, by strutting his feelings upon a stage, the right to expect silence about his personal affairs. [Lockhart's comment on this article in *Peter's Letters to His Kinsfolk,* II, 217, is given in section 5 of the Introduction.]

"Essays on the Lake School of Poetry"
July, 1818. III, 369, 370 Wilson[4]

Scott, Wordsworth, and Byron are placed on a triple throne. The poetry of Byron "is read as a dark, but still a divine revelation."

"Works of Charles Lamb"
August, 1818. III, 602 Wilson[5]

Byron is no Dante, but his *Manfred* shows he has the

[4] J. F. Ferrier's edition of Wilson's *Essays* [John Wilson, *Essays: Critical and Imaginative,* and *Noctes Ambrosianae,* each in four volumes (Edinburgh and London, William Blackwood, 1865, 4 vols.)], I, 387–92 correspond to pages 367–72 of this article.

[5] Ferrier, *ibid.,* I, 157 n., indicates that this article is Wilson's.

powers of a giant. "Above all, Scott and Byron want little, perhaps nothing, to become surpassing tragic dramatists."

"Mazeppa"
July, 1819. V, 429–32

The reviewer deems *Mazeppa* worthy of Byron's genius. But he objects to the Ode [on Venice] and the prose fragment [of a Novel] which Byron has added to make up his pamphlet. The first is "a foolish piece of heartless disloyal raving," and the second is "a little drivelling story."

Concluding note to "Crabbe's Tales of the Hall"
July, 1819. V, 483n. Wilson (?)[6]

Don Juan is mentioned in an ominous tone.

"Remarks on Don Juan"
August, 1819. V, 512–22 Lockhart, Wilson (?)[7]

This review contains the first bitter criticism of Byron's work. The poet's genius is admitted, but his morals are deplored. This very extraordinary new production "will remain to all ages a perpetual monument of the exalted intellect, and the depraved heart of one of the most remarkable men to whom this country has had the honour and the disgrace of giving birth." The immorality and the irreligion of the poem are indefensible, as is the attack on Lady Byron, an act "brutally, fiendishly, inexpiably mean."

Two notes in "To Correspondents" of November, 1819 (on back of No. XXXII, Vol. VI)

"N. N.'s remarks on Don Juan do great credit both to his

6 Wilson wrote the article proper: *Ibid.,* I, 400–401 correspond to pp. 470–71 of the piece; but he may not have had anything to do with the note.

7 E. H. Coleridge attributed this review to Wilson in Byron, *Poems,* VI, 213 and n. R. E. Prothero in Byron, *Letters and Journals,* IV, 385n., says that the article is *not* by Wilson. Macbeth in *Lockhart: A Critical Study,* 98, assigns the piece to Lockhart. Byron considered Wilson the author and wrote a reply.

head and heart. But we have already given our opinion of that poem; and though N. N. may have expressed his ideas better and more fully—we do not think he has added any thing new to what we said on the same subject. His letter is now lying for him with Messrs Cadell and Davies."

"It goes to our very heart to reject poetry by any of our fair Contributors. But non-insertion does not imply disapprobation. A Sonnet to Lord Byron, (M.A.C.) in particular, we unwillingly reject—for—though inaccurate in one line or two—it is exceedingly elegant."

"Remarks on Some of Our Late Numbers:
By a Liberal Whig"
December, 1819. VI, 288–89

"Metrodorus" does not much admire *Blackwood's* criticisms of Lord Byron's new poem"—i.e., *Don Juan*. "I cannot subscribe to the overstrained and somewhat hypocritical tone of abhorrence which it is the fashion to adopt with respect to it, on the alleged scores of morality and religion."

"Letter from the Ettrick Shepherd"
January, 1820. VI, 390 Lockhart[8]

Hogg reports that "Wastle" thinks *Don Juan* and *Anastatius* "likely to produce greater effects on the public mind than almost any things that our time has put forth." *Faublas* is mentioned as a source of *Anastatius,* a work which is speculated upon as being either Byron's or Hope's.

"Extracts from Mr Wastle's Diary. No. II."
June, 1820. VII, 317 Lockhart[9]

Byron is reported to be preparing a hit at *Blackwood's Magazine* in his new cantos of *Don Juan*. But "Wastle" points

8 The inclusion of stanzas of *The Mad Banker of Amsterdam* and the use of the pseudonym "Wastle," often employed by Lockhart, indicate that Lockhart must have been largely responsible for this piece.

9 M. Clive Hildyard, *Lockhart's Literary Criticism* (Oxford, Eng., Basil Blackwell, 1931), 154.

out, "He has always been praised in it, it appears to me, above his merits; and as to the attacks on his Beppo and Don Juan, surely he has too much sense to care for such trifles as these." ("Wastle" rejoices that the poet "has been abusing his old Jackall Hobhouse, for his conjunction with the radicals.")

"Lord Byron's Doge of Venice"
April, 1821. IX, 93–103 Wilson[10]

Marino Faliero "has the happiness to be distinguished . . . from too many of the productions of his Lordship's own genius, by uniform purity of thought and purpose. Without question, no such tragedy as this of Marino Faliero has appeared in English since the day when Otway also was inspired to his master-piece by the interests of a Venetian story and a Venetian conspiracy."

"Lord Byron and Pope"
May, 1821. IX, 227–33

In the review of Byron's *Letter on Pope,* "Y" advises Byron to stick to poetry, and if he "continues to live and to write, and will only abstain from Pamphlets and Magazines, he will be placed by universal acclamation far above" Pope, "the object of his present panegyric, and form a fourth star of a glorious constellation with Shakespeare, Milton, and Dryden."

"Letter to Lord Byron"
July, 1821. IX, 421–26

A humorous review of the letter by "John Bull" edited in this study. [See the next to the last paragraph in section 4 of the Introduction.]

"Continuation of Don Juan"
August (Part II), 1821. X, 107, 115

"Harry Franklin" hastens to put in a good word for *Don Juan* before "Christopher North" of *Blackwood's Magazine,*

[10] Byron, *Poems,* IV, 329.

who has "a confounded moral ill will at Byron," has a chance "to say one uncivil word on the subject." Cantos III, IV, and V "are not quite so naughty as their predecessors." They "will certainly help to redeem his poetical reputation from the effects of that lumbering mass of wagon-wheeled blank verse, 'The Doge.'" Finally, "North" receives warning that "it is harsh to ascribe to wicked motives what may be owing to the temptations of circumstances, or the headlong impulses of passion."

["This delightful letter," writes Dr. P. G. Trueblood in *The Flowering of Byron's Genius,* 40, 41, 42, "is urbane and tolerant." Its author "becomes the first reviewer to contradict the assertion of earlier critics that Byron's purpose in the poem is deliberate interest to corrupt morals."]

"Why are Poets Indifferent Critics?"
September, 1821. X, 183–86 T[homas] D[oubleday]

Byron on Pope, Byron and Milton. "When Lord Byron, in his Don Juan, first fairly introduced into English literature that fantastic mixture of the serious and comic . . . , many of our horror-stricken critics imagined, that the noble poet sat deliberately down to insult and confound the best feelings of our nature. Their very hair stood on end at such couplets as,

'They grieved for those that perish'd with the cutter,
And likewise for the bisquit-casks and butter.'

So difficult is it to reconcile one's self at first to any thing that is in opposition to a preconceived standard of taste."

"Lord Byron's Three New Tragedies"
(Including "Mr. Southey's Reply to
Lord Byron")
January, 1822. XI, 90–94 Lockhart[11]

Sardanapalus is judged an utter failure as a play, and not quite worthy of Byron as a poem. *The Foscari* "is totally inferior" to *Sardanapalus. Cain* contains "five or six passages

11 Macbeth, *Lockhart: A Critical Study,* 99.

of as fine poetry as Lord Byron ever wrote or will write; but, taken altogether, it is a wicked and blasphemous performance."

Southey, in his "Reply to Lord Byron," answers the "very venomous attack" which appears in a note to the tragedy of *The Foscari*. Lockhart thinks Southey's epithet of "Satanic School" ridiculous, but can find no defence for Byron's answering attack on the character of Southey's wife or his sarcasms about the Laureate's professional authorship.

"Lord Byron"
February, 1822. XI, 212–17

Condemnation by "Siluriensis" of Byron's tragedies. By way of introduction he says: "The cantos of Don Juan are of a light and playful description for the most part, and serious subjects may be therein treated with too great a degree of levity; but it cannot be denied that this work indicates prodigious powers of language, and mastership of rhyme." In a note to p. 213, "C[hristopher] N[orth]" calls the name "Satanic School of Poetry" "a miserable piece of monkish conceit."

"Letter from London"
February, 1822. XI, 237–38

Byron, "Shelly," and Hunt are to publish a journal: Byron's part in the "Holy Pisan Alliance" is deplored. The impending prosecution of *Cain* is mentioned.

"London Chit-Chat"
March, 1822. XI, 331

Byron's return to England is rumored. "The author of 'Amarynthus the Nympholept,' it is suspected, will be one of the contributors" to "the Pisan Journal" [i.e., *The Liberal*].

"Noctes Ambrosianae. No. I"
March, 1822. XI, 375, *361–*63, *378–*369

Lockhart (and Maginn?)[12]

Comments on Byron: the prosecution of *Cain* is a sign of

humbug; among other contemporary works, Byron's *Don Juan, Manfred,* and *Childe Harold* "will be much talked of a hundred years hence"; the "holy alliance of Pisa [between Byron, Shelley, and Leigh Hunt] will be a queer affair"; Byron's tragedies.

"Letter from Paddy"
April, 1822. XI, 461–65

The only poems of Byron which can lay the least claim to originality are the *Hours of Idleness* and the first two cantos of *Childe Harold.* Byron has been influenced by various writers including Coleridge and Wordsworth; now, under the influence of Leigh Hunt, he will write such verses as these:

"Lack-a-day! but I've grown wiser,
Since Mister Hunt has come to Pisar."

"He has become Italian in body and in soul."

"Cambridge Pamphlets—Irish Ball, &c. &c. &c."
June, 1822. XI, 740–41

The Quarterly and *Edinburgh Reviews* on Byron. Byron will sicken of Shelley and Hunt. "His later productions are successively his worst—his miserable tragedies have shewn, that when he is not allowed to rant about himself, he can do nothing—he has decidedly failed in the noblest class of poetry . . . ."

"The Quarterly Review. No. LIII"
July, 1822. XII, 97–99 Lockhart[13]

"Jeffrey was *afraid* to attack Lord Byron—and the editor of the Quarterly *dared* not censure a book which came from

[12] Ralph M. Wardle gives convincing proof of Lockhart's authorship of this first *Noctes.*—"The Authorship of the *Noctes Ambrosianae,*" *Modern Philology,* XLII, August, 1944, 10–11. See also Chew, *Byron in England,* 80. But I still think that Maginn had a share in the piece: see A. L. Strout, "Concerning the *Noctes Ambrosianae,*" *Modern Language Notes,* LI, December, 1936, 495–96.

[13] Hildyard, *Lockhart's Literary Criticism,* 155.

the shop of John Murray." Indeed, the advocate of the publisher of *Don Juan,* in the interest of piety, calls "for an alteration of the existing laws, to enable that gentleman and others, equally anxious about public morals, to fill their pockets by continuations of Don Juan, and new mysteries mocking the Scriptures." "Don Juan . . . is a pernicious book."

"The law has done its office. . . . We shall have no more Don Juans, or no more Cains, published by people who can liberally pay men of talent for prostituting their powers. . . . Such books will not be thrust on the trade by the overpowering influence of a great and rich publisher,—they must sneak in through some beggarly scoundrel, who will be mark for the cautious courage of the Society for the Suppression of Vice." Blackwood refused to sell a book without a publisher's name to it; "and though he has been abundantly laughed at for his squeamishness,—nay, Christopher, sneered at even in your own magazine, of which he is proprietor,—yet I shall ever assert, that in this refusal he acted as became a fair trader, and the father of a rising family."

"Noctes Ambrosianae. No. IV"

July, 1822. XII, 100–14 Maginn[14]

"Odoherty" and Byron meet at an inn in Pisa. Byron defends *Don Juan* and contends that in a religious poem *Cain,* "Speeches torn from the context, and misinterpreted by the malevolent or the weak-minded, may be made to prove what was directly contrary to the intention of the writer." "Odoherty" exclaims, "I had rather have written a page of Don Juan than a ton of Childe Harold." Byron asks for information of his enemies and friends.

14 Mrs. Oliphant, *Annals of a Publishing House,* I, 396. "A large portion of the preceding *Noctes* were [*sic*] written by Maginn, but that which followeth is entirely from his pen. It has so many actual points of *vraisemblance,* that even Byron himself is said to have exclaimed, after reading it, 'By Jupiter! the fellow has me down regularly, in black and white.' "—*Noctes Ambrosianae,* ed. by R. Shelton Mackenzie (New York, W. J. Widdleton, 5 vols.), I, 198 n.

"Odoherty on Werner"
December, 1822. XII, 710–19 Maginn (?)[15]

A review of Byron's dramas: in *Cain,* "Byron dared to measure himself with Milton, and came off as poorly as Belial might have done from a contest with Michael. . . . Thank God! Cain was abandoned to the Radicals—and thank God, it was too radically dull to be popular even among them."

"Odoherty" declares *Werner* a play in which Byron has added nothing to the original, one of Miss Lee's *Canterbury Tales.* "My Lord Byron has no sort of title, none in the world, to be considered as having acted the part of a poet in the concoction and execution of *his* Werner."

"On the Cockney School. No. VII. Hunt's Art of Love"
December, 1822. XII, 781 Lockhart (?)[16]

"What, in the name of Katterfelto, can Byron mean by patronizing a Cockney? . . . As to Don Juan and Cain, we pardon you them; but this sin is beyond the reach of our forgiveness . . . ."

"Tickler on Werner"
December, 1822. XII, 782–85

"Tickler" defends Byron from the charge of plagiarism but thinks the character of Werner poorly conceived, and poorly executed. Byron's blank verse is poor. "On the whole, Werner is not more than a degree or two above Mirandola—and rather a stupid affair."

"Byron's Heaven and Earth"
January, 1823. XIII, 72–77 Wilson[17]

Byron's *Heaven and Earth* is judged far superior to Moore's

[15] Byron, *Poems,* V, 326–27. Wardle ("Who Was Morgan Odoherty?" *PMLA,* LVIII, September, 1943) says the authorship of the piece is not known.

[16] Hildyard, *Lockhart's Literary Criticism,* 157, says that Lockhart's share in the article is undetermined.

[17] In a review of Irving's *Heaven and Hell,* September, 1823, known to be Wilson's, the opening sentence runs: "We laid before our readers ample extracts from Lord Byron's Heaven and Earth," etc. See also Byron, *Poems,* V, 282.

Love of the Angels. "Moore writes with a crow-quill. . . . Byron writes with an eagle's plume." "The great power of this 'Mystery' is in its fearless and daring simplicity."

"The Candid. No. I"
January, 1823. XIII, 108–24 Wilson (?)[18]
A discussion by "R. S." of "that Paltry Periodical of Pisa" [i.e., *The Liberal*].

"The Candid. No. II"
March, 1823. XIII, 261–75 Wilson (?)
"R. S." strongly condemns "this poetic scrap" Byron's *Heaven and Earth* along with all the other contents of *The Liberal.*

"On the Scotch Character—By a Flunky"
March, 1823. XIII, 365–67 Wilson[19]
Byron has hired two or three Cockneys as "menial servants." A rip-snorting attack on Leigh Hunt, which, Walter Scott feared, might result in a duel.

"The Age of Bronze"
April, 1823. XIII, 457–60 Lockhart (?)[20]
An anonymous Cockney is upbraided for trying to pass off the doggrel *Age of Bronze* as his.

"Noctes Ambrosianae. No. VIII"
May, 1823. XIII, 607, 611
The last issue of *The Liberal* "contains *not one* line of Byron's." The last two cantos of *Don Juan* are begging for a publisher. Hogg, a consistent champion of Byron in the *Noctes,* says of these last two cantos, "They're extraordinary

18 This article contains the criticisms of Byron's *Heaven and Earth* and of Moore's *Love of the Angels,* both of which are by Wilson.

19 Mrs. Oliphant, *Annals of a Publishing House,* I, 274–76. Compare Mrs. Gordon, *Christopher North,* 260.

20 Hildyard, *Lockhart's Literary Criticism,* 157, says Lockhart's share in the article is undetermined.

clever—they're better even than the twa first; but that mischievous Constitutional Association will not let ony body daur to print them. And, after all, it's maybe as weel sae, for they're gay wicked, I must alloo; and yet, it's amaist a pity."

"Tickler on the New Cantos of Don Juan"
(Canto VI, VII, VIII)
July, 1823. XIV, 88–92 Maginn and Lockhart[21]
A violent attack leading to the conclusion: "I don't remember anything so complete as the recent fall of Lord Byron's literary name." "Alas! Poor Byron! Not ten times a-day . . . but ten times a-page, as I wandered over the intense and incredible stupidities of this duodecimo, was the departed spirit of the genius of Childe Harold saluted with this exclamation." In these cantos "we are wallowing in a sty of mere filth." "Tickler" declares that some of the verses "have all the appearance of having been interpolated by the King of the Cockneys." A long discussion of the influence of *Faublas* appears on p. 90.

"Noctes Ambrosianae. No. X"
July, 1823. XIV, 103–104 Maginn[22]
Byron has sunk to be "a scribbler in a dirty magazine [*The Liberal*], and a patron of the Hunts!" Christian in *The Island* lacks originality.

"Letters of Timothy Tickler, Esq. No. VIII"
August, 1823. XIV, 214–18 Lockhart and Maginn[22]
On infamous books when pirated. "Tickler" rejoices that Lord Eldon's recent decision, besides keeping out of the mar-

21 "Lockhart wrote to Blackwood: 'I have run over the Doctor [i.e., Maginn] and added a few pages as you see. . . . I really have not read the poem, but dipping here and there it seems worthy of all that Maginn says' . . . . Maginn, incensed that Byron should have allowed his new instalment of *Don Juan* to be published by John Hunt, brother of 'King Leigh,' slashed at it relentlessly."—Ralph M. Wardle, " 'Timothy Tickler's' Irish Blood," *The Review of English Studies*, XVIII, October, 1942, 487.

22 *Ibid.*, 487–88.

ket books of wicked cleverness, makes any respectable publisher unwilling to venture to produce *Don Juan,* the work of a "successful profligate of genius."

"Odoherty on Don Juan, Cantos IX. X. XI"
September, 1823. XIV, 282–93 Lockhart[23]

"Odoherty" accuses "Tickler" and "North" of humbug. Byron, he declares, is far from "his dotage." Some blame, to be sure, attaches to *Don Juan:* "Blame Don Juan; blame Faublas; blame Candide; but blame them for what really is deserving of blame. Stick to your good old rule—abuse Wickedness, but acknowledge Wit."

"I maintain, and have always maintained, that Don Juan is, without exception, the first of Lord Byron's works. It is by far the most original in point of *conception.* It is decidedly original in point of *tone.* . . . It contains the finest specimens of serious poetry he has ever written; and it contains the finest specimens of ludicrous poetry that our age has witnessed. . . . Don Juan is destined to hold a permanent rank in the literature of our country." The morality of the poem is defended: "Is it *more* obscene than Tom Jones?—Is it *more* blasphemous than Voltaire's novels? In point of fact, it is not within fifty miles of either of them: and as to obscenity, there is more of that in the pious Richardson's pious Pamela, than in all the novels and poems that have been written since."

"Letters of Timothy Tickler, Esq. No. X"
September, 1823. XIV, 314 Lockhart[24]

"Tickler" comments on Byron's break with Leigh Hunt.

[23] Lockhart wrote Blackwood: "Don Juan—these cantos are far better than the last three. Shall I say so?"—Mrs. Oliphant, *Annals of a Publishing House,* I, 208. The publisher had in turn written John Wilson: "Write to me what you think of the article [by Lockhart], as I fear it is apt to startle weak minds."—Mrs. Gordon, *Christopher North,* 268. Hildyard, *Lockhart's Literary Criticism,* 155, assigns the piece to Lockhart also.

[24] Mrs. Gordon, *Christopher North,* 266; Hildyard, *Lockhart's Literary Criticism,* 155.

"Remarks on Mr. Sullivan's Dramatic Poems"
June, 1824. XV, 675 Maginn[25]

"Poetry, it is vain to deny it, is becoming a drug of the most opium-like propensities. Lord Byron—light lie the stones upon his bones—fed us full of horrors. We had dark-eyed fellows, with bushy eyebrows, white foreheads, gloomy cogitations, deep amorosities, and a decided penchant for cutting throats, and easing honest way-farers of the contents of their purses. These neat gentlemen were served up to us in all possible varieties. Even Don Juan was but a Childe Harold doing vagaries, like John Kemble acting Mirabel. No constitution could long stand doses of this kind; and accordingly the stomach of that worthy old gentlewoman, the Public, rejected them at last. It was a pity; for, though there was no variety, the very worst of his lordship's *esquisses* displayed the hand of no ordinary man. We always except his tragedies, which were sad concerns—*lachrymosa poemata,* in every sense but one. However, he knocked up poetry more completely than any man of our day."

"Lord Byron"
June, 1824. XV, 696–701

An anonymous contributor tells of his visit with Byron at Genoa, representing the poet favorably.

"Noctes Ambrosianae. No. XV"
June, 1824. XV, 709–19 Maginn, Lockhart (?)[26]

Byron's Memoirs including his "Dictionary" receive men-

[25] Wardle, "Who Was Morgan Odoherty?" *PMLA,* LVIII, September, 1943, 725.

[26] Mackenzie assigns to Maginn, *Noctes Ambrosianae,* I, 477 n. Wardle writes: "Though I suspect that Lockhart had a main share in the paper, I cannot prove it." My own opinion is that since Maginn read Byron's Memoirs before their destruction in London, he presumably had a considerable share in the production; but Wardle's excellent account of this *Noctes* should be read entire: "The Authorship of the *Noctes Ambrosianae", Modern Philology,* XLII, August, 1944, 13–14. Lockhart's letter to Maginn concerning this *Noctes,* a letter written in May or June, 1824, will be found in Appendix C.

tion. "Tickler" praises, "Odoherty" condemns the poet and his works. But the latter praises Byron's prose superlatively: ". . . Byron never could versify . . . his Memoirs and his private letters are the only things of his, that I have ever seen, that gave me, in the least degree, the notion of a fine creature enjoying the full and unconstrained swing of his faculties. . . .

"I tell you, Byron's prose works, when they are printed, will decidedly fling his verse into total oblivion. You, sir, that have merely read his hide-bound, dry, barking, absurd, ungrammatical cantos of Don Juan, and judge from them of Byron's powers as a satirist, are in the most pitiable position imaginable. One thumping paragraph of a good honest thorough-going letter of his to Douglas Kinnaird, or Murray in the olden time, is worth five ton of that material."

Hogg places himself and Byron at the head of writers. "Odoherty" sings a lament for Byron.

"Deaths"
June, 1824. XV, 736

Death notice of Byron.

"Lord Byron's Conversations"
November, 1824. XVI, 530–40 Lockhart (?)[27]

The inexcusable destruction of Byron's Memoirs "has served the cause of hypocrisy much more than that of virtue." In this double review of Medwin's work, the tone towards Byron is friendly, but Medwin is treated "with coolness and contempt."

"Captain Medwin's account of his lordship's marriage and separation, is . . . in substance true;—but some of the incidents are much better told by the poet in Don Juan, which, however, we have, of course, too much regard for the morality of *our* readers to quote; but we refer those who dare venture on the experiment, to the first canto."

27 Hildyard, *Lockhart's Literary Criticism,* 155, says the authorship is doubtful.

"Southey and Byron"
December, 1824. XVI, 711–15 Lockhart (?)[27]

Byron is declared "this great and godlike Poet of England." Southey is warned that the world will not approve his prolonging "the existence of feelings which never ought to have existed at all." There follows Southey's answer to the "base and blundering folly of this Captain Medwin."

"Lord Byron"[28]
February, 1825. XVII, 131–51

The reviewer begins by considering Byron's treatment in contemporary periodicals and exultingly remarks that *Blackwood's Magazine* never, "at any period of our career, either neglected or ill-treated the great poet who is now no more."

This article, a formal review of Byron's life, discusses his personal qualities with sympathy and forbearance: "We shall, like all others who say anything about Lord Byron, begin *sans apologie* with his personal character." The poet's genius receives whole-hearted admiration, especially as regards *Don Juan.* The review proceeds with extracts from Sir Egerton Brydges's *Letters on the Character and Genius of Lord Byron,* from "Dallas's book, utterly feeble and drivelling as it is," and from Count Gamba's *A Narrative of Lord Byron's Last Journey to Greece,* with passing reference to Hobhouse and Medwin. Finally, Byron's espousal of the Greek cause is pronounced "clear, high, and glorious throughout."

"Noctes Ambrosianae. No. XIX"
March, 1825. XVII, 376 Wilson[29]

Hogg says of Byron, "Many a cruel thing has been uttered against him, and I wish, Mr. North, you would vindicate him, now that his hand is cauld." "North" says, "The character of one of the greatest poets the world ever saw, in a very few years, will be discerned in the clear light of truth."

28 Macbeth, *Lockhart: A Critical Study,* 99, assigns to Lockhart. Chew, *Byron in England,* 210n., attributes to Wilson.

29 This is the first of the *Noctes* that Ferrier includes in his edition.

"Analytical Essays on the Modern English Drama. No. III. On Babington, a Tragedy"
July, 1825. XVIII, 119 Wilson (?)

Scott, Byron, Coleridge, Baillie, Milman, Wilson, and Shelley have "all written tragedies which may be compared, without obscuration of their power, with the compositions of our best dramatic writers. De Montfort, Basil, The Remorse, Sardanapalus, Cain, Fazio, The City of the Plague, The Cenci—Do they contain less poetry, less passion, less pathos, than the dramas of Ford or Massinger? In our opinion infinitely more."

"Parry's Last Days of Lord Byron"
August, 1825. XVIII, 137–55

"We opened this volume with no very sanguine expectations either of instruction or of amusement. Medwin, Gamba, Dallas, had all published, and had all disappointed us most grievously. The last named gentleman betrayed, in his own style of writing, the unpleasant fact, that he was an extremely dull person. The weakness, the puerile imbecility of Count Gamba's mind, was at once made manifest in the same manner. . . . The lieutenant of light dragoons came out of the business with a still worse grace. He certainly proved himself to be a blockhead." A fourth author, Colonel Leicester Stanhope, was a fourth disappointment: "a crack-brained enthusiast of the regular Bentham breed."

Parry's book is generously reviewed, the same considerate sympathy being shown to him that he showed to Byron in his book. A sketch is given of Byron's connection with the Greek cause. The cause itself, however, is not admired: "it cost England Byron, at seven-and-thirty!"

2. *Parodies and Travesties of Byron's Works: Poems on Byron*

May, 1818. III, 201–204

"Fragment of a Fifth Canto of Childe Harold's Pilgrimage." Dedicated to Mr. H[unt]., with notes chiefly written by him. These verses follow one of "Z.'s" letters to Leigh Hunt.

July, 1819. V, 434–39

"John Gilpin and Mazeppa."[30] "John Gilpin" is the prototype of "Mazeppa": Gilpin's ride is pronounced the more hazardous.

November, 1819. VI, 194–95

"Don Juan Unread." Maginn.[31] An amusing parody of Wordsworth's "Yarrow Unvisited," containing hits at Byron, the Cockneys, and others.

May, 1820. VII, 186–87

" 'Luctus' on the Death of Donnelly." Lockhart (?).[32] "Childe Daniel," accompanied by notes lamenting Sir Daniel Donnelly, Late Champion of Ireland, by Lord Byron, is the first of several parodies of contemporary poets.

July, 1820. VII, 437–41

"John and Joan. A New Poem." The second canto of "Josiah Shufflebotham's" piece, intended to serve "as a sort of antidote or counter charm, for this giddy generation, to the dangerous maxims set forth" in *Don Juan.*

30 E. H. Coleridge, in Byron, *Poetry,* IV, 203, attributes the contribution to Maginn; but R. M. Wardle, in "Who Was Morgan Odoherty?" *PMLA,* LVIII, September, 1943, 717, shows that Maginn did not contribute to *Maga* before November, 1819.

31 Wardle considers this article "unquestionably Maginn's." He points out that it is reprinted in R. Shelton Mackenzie's *Miscellaneous Writings of the Late Dr. Maginn* (New York, Redfield, 1857, 5 vols.); reprinted as Maginn's in John Murray's seventeen-volume edition of Byron (1832–33), XV; and acknowledged by Maginn in a prefatory letter in his "Letter from M. Mullion," *Blackwood's Magazine,* XII, August, 1822, 167.

See Ralph M. Wardle's doctoral thesis (Harvard University, 1940), *William Maginn and Blackwood's Magazine,* 356.

32 Hildyard, *Lockhart's Literary Criticism,* 156, lists this as one of the articles in *Maga* "in which Lockhart's share is undetermined." See also Wardle, "Who Was Morgan Odoherty?" *PMLA,* LVIII, September, 1943, 720, especially n. 22.

August, 1820. VII, 477–81

"Daniel O'Rourke, An Epic Poem, in Six Cantos. By Fagarty O'Fogarty. Canto I." Dr. Gosnell.[33] The poem is in "a metre now immortalized by Byron."

> "Although some gentlemen decry Don Juan,
> And shun him as a most indecent fellow,
> I still believe that of our poems, few, one
> Will find in harmony so rich and mellow."

(Other cantos follow to the sixth, which appears in the magazine of November, 1821, X, 429–37. "O'Fogarty" refers to *Don Juan* once more, in the second stanza:

> "The metre that I write in, I am told,
> Has lately got much into disrepute,
> Since the last cantos of the Don were roll'd
> Forth on the world, good morals to pollute.")

May, 1821. IX, 136, 137

"Familiar Letter from the Adjutant." Maginn (?).[34] Two parodies of Byron: "The Galiongee" and "Childe Paddy's banishment to New Holland."

January, 1822. XI, 116–19

"New-Year's Day Congratulations." Various contemporary poets compliment *Maga* at the new year. ". . . Here comes Byron with his famous letter on our Magazine." A "Rhyming Salutation" follows. Stanza 5 runs:

> "You think I hate you, for you cut me hard,
> And give me a sound drubbing now and then . . .
> Your approbation is my best reward;
> And to your fiat I do bow me when
> You think it meet—I believe you have never seen
> My famous letter on your Magazine?"

33 Maginn sent in separate cantos, sometimes added prefaces, and told Blackwood that the verse was by "Dr. Gosnell, Ross Carbery, Co. Cork"; see Wardle's thesis, *William Maginn* and *Blackwood's Magazine,* 343–45.

34 Chew, *Byron in England,* 111 n.

February, 1822. XI, 161–65

"Another Ladleful from the Devil's Punch Bowl." "Lord Byron's Combolio" with notes. "A metrical advertisement of all Lord Byron's works" in light verse.

March, 1822. XI, 376–*359

"Noctes Ambrosianae. No. I." Lockhart (and Maginn?).[35] A rhymed version of the "Letter from Lord Byron to Mr. Murray," in which Byron seeks to divert attacks from Murray to himself.

April, 1822. XI, 456–60

"Critique on Lord Byron."[36] A humorous criticism, in rhyme, of Byron's works, by "Palaemon."

> ". . . 'Twould be wrong, noble Bard,
> Oh! permit me to tell ye,
> To establish a league with Leigh
> Hunt and Byshe Shelley . . . ."

July, 1822. XII, 79

"Metricum Symposium Ambrosianum . . ." Maginn (?). Among contemporary authors, Byron first receives mention:

> "A bumper, my boys! Here's the
> profligate Baron . . .
> His Lordship, who, in the dull
> play the Foscari,
> Wrote worse than e'er Cockneyland's
> regent, mild Barry,
> And whose fame and whose genius

[35] See n. 12 and n. 14 above.

[36] Chew, *Byron in England,* 116, attributes this piece to Maginn, and it is reprinted in Mackenzie's *Miscellaneous Writings of the late Dr. Maginn;* but Wardle finds no evidence of authorship. Indeed, Maginn wrote Blackwood, April 29, 1822, "I have not been able to do anything worth mentioning for you these some weeks."—Wardle's thesis, *William Maginn in Blackwood's Magazine,* 382.

came down to their Zero
In the robberies and wretchedness
of Faliero . . .
Who spouts out more venom than
Amphisboena . . . ."

July, 1822. XII, 113
"Noctes Ambrosianae. No. IV." Maginn.[35] Byron, introduced into this *Noctes,* sings a parody of "There's not a Joy that Life can give."

March, 1823. XIII, 384
"Noctes Ambrosianae, No. VII." Maginn.[37] "On the head of George Buchanan": a parody of Byron's "On the star of 'The Legion of Honour' " (1816).

June, 1824. XV, 717–18
"Noctes Ambrosianae. No. XV." "Odoherty" sings a "Lament for Lord Byron"—the work probably of Maginn.[37]

July, 1824. XVI, 115–16
"Letters of Timothy Tickler, Esq. No. XVI."[38] A sharp attack in verse on "Byron's Chapter" in the *John Bull Magazine.*

May, 1825. XVII, between pp. 504 and 505
"Number a Hundred. A New Song, by Christopher North, Esq. himself." A reference to Byron and "the Cockneys":

". . . Even Byron, though using their
monarch as tool,
Call'd them after OUR nickname, the
base Cockney-School."

37 See Wardle, "The Authorship of the *Noctes Ambrosianae,*" *Modern Philology,* XLII, August, 1944, 12, 14.

38 Wardle considers this poem "almost certainly not Maginn's." See " 'Timothy Tickler's' Irish Blood," *The Review of English Studies,* XVIII, October, 1942, 489.

3. *Brief References to Byron and his Works*

April, 1817. I, 33

"On Sitting below the Salt." Byron, with Scott and Southey, displays erudition.

April, 1817. I, 76

"Review.—Harold the Dauntless." Byron and other poets have, "each in one instance," imitated Scott.

June, 1817. I, 284

"Review.—Lalla Rookh." Wilson.[39] Moore's Azim in *Lalla Rookh* resembles Byron's heroes.

July, 1817. I, 388–89, 394

"Marlow's Tragical History of Dr. Faustus." Wilson.[40] A general resemblance between Marlowe's *Dr. Faustus* and Byron's *Manfred* is noted. "Many glorious works of the mighty dead" are pronounced superior to the best poems which Byron's "powerful genius" has yet produced.

October, 1817. II, 7, 15

"Observations on Coleridge's Biographia Literaria." Wilson.[41] Byron speaks of himself in his works, but in such a way that "we listen with a kind of mysterious dread to the tones of a Being whom we scarcely believe to be kindred to ourselves, while he sounds the depths of our nature, and illuminates them with the lightnings of his genius." Byron admires *Christabel.*

October, 1817. II, 30n.

"Analytical Essays on the Early English Dramatists. No. II. *Edward II.*—Marlow." Wilson.[42] Refutation of the *Edinburgh Review* on *Manfred.*

39 Champneys, *Patmore,* II, 433.

40 Mrs. Oliphant, *Annals of a Publishing House,* I, 264; Chew, *Byron in England,* 113n.; and Byron, *Poems,* IV, 80.

41 Mrs. Oliphant, *Annals of a Publishing House,* I, 262, 263, 264.

42 *Ibid.,* I, 264.

October, 1817. II, 38, 40–41

"On the Cockney School of Poetry. No. I." Lockhart.[43] Satirical quotation from Cornelius Webb, who calls Byron "our England's Dante." Leigh Hunt is scorned for assuming to dedicate his *Rimini* to Lord Byron.

November, 1817. II, 187

"Some Account of the late John Finlay, with Specimens of his Poetry." Wilson.[44] Before the days of Campbell, Scott, Byron, and Joanna Baillie, Scotland could boast little of modern poets.

November, 1817. II, 196–98

"On the Cockney School of Poetry. No. II." Lockhart.[45] Byron's treatment of incest in *Manfred* and *Parisina* is not as objectionable as Hunt's treatment of it in *Rimini.*

December, 1817. II, 270

"Remarks on Godwin's New Novel, Mandeville." Lockhart.[46] "Two great English writers of the present day," Byron and Godwin, like their master Dante, have given birth to a set of terrible personifications.

December, 1817. II, 287

"To the Reviewer of Coleridge's Biographia Literaria, in Blackwood's Magazine for October." Another mention is made of Byron's admiration for *Christabel.*

January, 1818. II, 415

"Letter from Z. to Mr. Leigh Hunt." Lockhart.[47] "Z.," says Hunt is "a poet vastly inferior to Wordsworth, Byron, and Moore."

February, 1818. II, 569

"Notices of the Acted Drama in London. No. II." *The*

43 Macbeth, *Lockhart: A Critical Study,* 182.

44 Mrs. Gordon, *Christopher North,* 68 n., 101 n.

45 Macbeth, *Lockhart: A Critical Study,* 182.

46 Hildyard, *Lockhart's Literary Criticism,* 153.

47 Macbeth, *Lockhart: A Critical Study,* 182.

Bride of Abydos, at Drury Lane, is a tattered representation of Byron's poem.

April, 1818. III, 73–74
"Notice of Hazlitt's Lectures on English Poetry." P. G. Patmore.[48] Though Byron is selfish and self-absorbed, "in vigour of style, and force of conception, he surpasses every poet of the present day."

June, 1818. III, 297
"Thoughts on Public Feeling." Lockhart.[49] Byron is "a lamentable and unnatural exception" to the rule that the greatest poets of a nation express the character of its people.

August, 1818. III, 533
"Note on Odoherty and his Imitators." Byron is facetiously listed as an imitator of "Odoherty."

October, 1818. II, 1–5
"Remarks on the Poetry of Thomas Moore." Lockhart.[50] Honors have descended on Byron, Wordsworth, and Campbell. Moore has tried to compete with Byron. Byron's representation of women is mentioned.

October, 1818. IV, 16
"D'Israeli on the Literary Character." Byron was influenced in childhood by Rycaut's folio of Turkish History.

December, 1818. IV, 279
"The Chateau of Coppet." Byron's visit to Madame de Staël receives mention.

January, 1819. IV, 445
"Notices of the Acted Drama in London." Byron is mentioned as a potential dramatist.

48 Champneys, *Patmore,* II, 433–34.
49 Hildyard, *Lockhart's Literary Criticism,* 153.
50 *Ibid.*

March, 1819. IV, 695

"Notice of a Perpetual Kalendar." Byron's sublime *Apostrophe to the Ocean* is mentioned.

June, 1819. V, 274

"Rosalind and Helen, a Modern Eclogue." Wilson.[51] Shelley "in nerve and pith of conception approaches more nearly to Scott and Byron than any other of their contemporaries."

June, 1819. V, 286

"Letter from Mr. Odoherty, enclosing the third part of Christabel." D. M. Moir.[52] "Odoherty" threatens to publish *his Don Juan.*

July, 1819. V, 433

"Letter from Mr. Odoherty, enclosing Three Articles."[53] The postscript runs: "Give my compliments to Mr. Murray. I see he has taken my hint about Don Juan. Well, I give him a month's law; and if he allows that time to elapse, you shall certainly see *my Don Juan* in the course of a week after."

August, 1819. V, 597

"The true and authentic Account of the Twelfth of August, 1819." Wilson, Lockhart, Capt. Thomas Hamilton (?).[54] *Don Juan* is silently sent to the devil.

September, 1819. V, 627

"The Tent." Wilson (?).[55] *Don Juan* (in merest passing mention) is "boldly dashed at."

51 See A. L. Strout, *"Maga,* Champion of Shelley," *Studies in Philology,* XXIX, January, 1932, 99 and notes. See also E. Dowden, *Life of Shelley* (London, Kegan Paul, Trench & Co., 1886, 2 vols.), II, 203.

52 See A. L. Strout, "S. T. Coleridge and John Wilson of *Blackwood's Magazine," PMLA,* XLVIII, March, 1933, 111 and notes.

53 See n. 30 above.

54 These articles are apparently a composite affair, largely by Wilson, Lockhart, and Captain Thomas Hamilton, the originator of "Odoherty."

55 Lang, *Life of Lockhart,* I, 252, attributes the "Kirk of Shotts" to Wilson. See the preceding note.

September, 1819. V, 640

"Cockney Poetry and Cockney Politics." Leigh Hunt is not fit to associate with Byron, Scott, and Wordsworth.

October, 1819. VI, 70

"On the Cockney School of Poetry. No. VI." Lockhart (?).[56] Hunt is ridiculed for addressing "my dear Byron."

November, 1819. VI, 154

"Nugae Canorae; by Charles Lloyd." Wilson (?). Scott, Wordsworth, Southey, Coleridge, Campbell, and Byron are listed as great poets.

December, 1819. VI, 233

"Literary Pocket-Book." Wilson (?). "Gruff old General Izzard" [i.e., the "Z." of *Maga*] is at Vienna with Lord Byron and Mr. Moore.

March, 1820. VI, 647

"A Sicilian Story, with other Poems; by Barry Cornwall." "Cornwall's" Don Diego is a sort of cousin of Don Juan.

March, 1820. VI, 677

"Remarks on the Diversity of Genius." The writer quotes Jeffrey's opinion that Byron surpasses in power of expression and in unextinguishable energy of sentiment Scott, Campbell, Crabbe, and Moore.

April, 1820. VII, 34

"Essay on Song Writing." Byron's *Hebrew Melodies* "are neither Hebrew nor melodies; but his Lordship can well afford to suffer for the misnomer."

May, 1820. VII, 206

"Wordsworth's River Duddon." Wilson (?). The productions of Scott, and Byron, and Wordsworth, and Southey, and Coleridge are "kindred to each other by their part in the common Soul and Thought of the time that has witnessed

[56] Hildyard, *Lockhart's Literary Criticism,* 156, says the authorship is doubtful.

their birth." Byron's fame is great whether or not acknowledged by critics.

June, 1820. VII, 238–40

"The Faustus of Goethe." Lockhart.[57] *Faustus* is discussed as the source of Byron's *Manfred:* "Lord Byron's obligations to Faustus . . . are not as great as he [Goethe] imagines."

August, 1820. VII, 520

"Advice to Julia. A Letter in Rhyme." Lockhart.[58] Moore is inferior to Byron in "every essential of poetry and feeling." Moore's immorality is by far the more disgusting of the two.

January, 1821. VIII, 458

"The Earthquake." "In some of Lord Byron's more recent productions, his Lordship has renounced the fierce bravadoing tone with which he first fired ardent souls, and, in Don Juan, he evidently inclines more towards sarcasm, reflection and tears."

February, 1821. VIII, 542

"Epistle from Odoherty."[59] "Odoherty" still emphasizes his competition with Byron: "If Byron's Third Canto of Juan does not come out within a month, the public will have to decide, which of us is the better writer, the projector, or the continuator."

April, 1821. IX, 60, 63

"Hymn to Christopher North, Esq." Maginn.[60] A parody of Southey's "Vision of Judgment."

> ". . . Drunk as a lord I shall get,
>   drunk as his lordship of Byron,*
> When he sat boozing in Thebes with
>   the sixbottle Solyman Pacha."

[57] *Ibid.,* 154; also Lang, *Life of Lockhart,* I, 245.

[58] Hildyard, *Lockhart's Literary Criticism,* 154.

[59] The "Epistle" "is certainly not Maginn's."—R. M. Wardle, "Who Was Morgan Odoherty," *PMLA,* LVIII, September, 1943, 721.

[60] Mrs. Oliphant, *Annals of a Publishing House,* I, 375.

*"Lord Byron commemorates this adventure in a note on one of his poems, Childe Harold, I believe."

May, 1821. IX, 132–33

"Familiar Letter from the Adjutant." Maginn (?).[61] "Odoherty" discusses Byron, remarking on "Count Manfred, alias Dr. Faustus, jun." and other poems.

June, 1821. IX, 284

"On the alleged Decline of Dramatic Writing." T[homas] D[oubleday]. Byron on *The School for Scandal.*

September, 1821. X, 200–206

"Familiar Epistles to Christopher North, from an Old Friend with a New Face. Letter II. On Anastatius. By Lord Byron." The author in a laborious argument seeks to prove Byron the author of *Anastatius.*

October, 1821. X, 286

"Letter from A. S. Trott, Esq." Maginn.[62] "Leigh Hunt is most horribly annoyed at not being either praised or abused in *Don Juan.*"

October, 1821. X, 295–98

"Chaucer and Don Juan." Chaucer, long before Byron, employed a serio-comic style.

61 Chew, *Byron in England,* 111 n. Wardle thinks either Maginn or Hamilton, or both, may have written the piece.—"Who Was Morgan Odoherty?" *PMLA,* LVIII, September, 1943, 722.

62 Wardle says that Maginn's authorship is proved by a letter from Gerald Griffin to his brother in November, 1824: "[Maginn] attacked Banim . . . , but that's all forgot long since. Hazlitt praised Banim in the London Magazine and of course rendered it imperative on Blackwood to abuse him."—*The Works of Gerald Griffin,* ed. by Daniel Griffin (London, 1843, 2 vols.), I, 181.

Note that the "Letter from Trott" derides Banim, mentions Hazlitt's praise of him, and is the only reference to Banim indexed in *Blackwood's* previous to November, 1824. Note also that it mentions the London journalists' unsympathetic reporting of the King's visit to Ireland, stressed in Maginn's article of that name—an article acknowledged by Maginn in a letter to Blackwood of September 9, 1821.—Wardle's thesis, *William Maginn and Blackwood's Magazine,* 348.

November, 1821. X, 440

"Brief Abstract of Mr. O'Fogarty's Journal." Byron's praise of *Christabel* is quoted.

November, 1821. X, 474, 475

"Rouge et Noir." "Lord Byron has failed in dramatic writing, the first in dignity, by the want of . . . compression. The bonds of rhyme seem essential to his vigour. Blank-verse suffers him to wander away into endless diffusion."

December, 1821. X, 558, 560

"A Midsummer Night's Dream." A reference is made to the Bowles-Byron controversy. Byron is called "his Ex-Lordship of Newstead."

December, 1821. X, 579

"The Literary Pocket-Book." Wilson (?). "Put Byron, Wordsworth, Crabbe, Scott, and Southey, aside, and all the other great living poets seem to us one flock of sheep."

December, 1821. (Part II), X, 679–80

"Rise, Progress, Decline, and Fall of the Edinburgh Review." Byron's treatment in the *Edinburgh Review*.

December, 1821. X, 730–33, 740

"Lyndsay's Dramas of the Ancient World." Lord Byron as a dramatist: his *Cain* and *Sardanapalus, Manfred* and *Marino Faliero*. "Byron's Manfred is a magnificent drama—and his Doge is stately and austere."

January, 1822. XI, *viii*

"Preface." Byron's letter "on or to" the Editor of *Blackwood's Magazine* is mentioned.

January, 1822. XI, 62, 63–65

"Moore's Irish Melodies." Byron and the *Literary Gazette*. Byron and Moore.

February, 1822. XI, 138
"On the Genius and Character of Rousseau." Wilson (?).[63] Moore as a critic of Byron.

February, 1822. XI, 154, 157
"How far is Poetry an Art?" T[homas] D[oubleday]. Byronic schools of poetry. Byron employed materials seen in his travels.

March, 1822. XI, 268
"Milman's Martyr of Antioch." Byron's poetical growth.

March, 1822. XI, 347–48
"Rhapsodies over a Punch-Bowl. No. I." Byron's *Letter to Bowles* is a "prime specimen of humbug."

April, 1822. XI, 347–48
"On the Drama." "Byron will never write a tragedy." Byron is an aristocrat.

May, 1822. XI, 608–11
"Noctes Ambrosianae. No. III." Maginn (?).[64] Mention of the Byron-Jeffrey feud.

June, 1822. XI, 669
"Lights and Shadows of Scottish Life." Comments on Byron's late productions.

July, 1822. XII, 58
"Letter from a 'Gentleman of the Press.' " Maginn.[65] "Jef-

[63] On I know not what authority, Hugo Struve assigns the article to Wilson in *John Wilson als Kritiker* (Berlin, University of Berlin, 1921), 3.

[64] Mackenzie assigns "a large portion" of this production to Maginn. —*Noctes Ambrosianae,* I, 198n.

[65] Maginn acknowledges this article in a letter to Blackwood of June 9, 1822: "You got yesterday . . . a sort of quiz matter on which you have already decided. If you approve of it . . . , you can head this 'Review of the concluding article of No. 64 of *The* Magazine.' " (Cf. the footnote on the first page of the *Letter:* "Mr. T. alludes to the concluding article of our sixty-fourth Number . . . ."—Wardle's thesis, *William Maginn and Blackwood's Magazine,* 352.

frey, in one of his thousand-and-one slanderous articles, told Lord Byron that he ought to give up poetry—for that Nature never intended him to be a poet. Did anybody believe the smallest of critics? Nobody with more brains than a titmouse."

August, 1822. XII, 153
"The Quarterly Review. No. LIII." A note on Lockhart's article of July, 1822, considered in the preceding first section.

August, 1822. XII, 159–62
"Hazlitt's Table-Talk." Hazlitt credits Byron's popularity to his nobility.

August, 1822. XII, 176
"Wordsworth's Sonnets and Memorials." Wilson.[66] Byron's poetical debt to Wordsworth.

September, 1822. XII, 377
"Noctes Ambrosianae. No. V." Reference to Byron's swimming.

December, 1822. XII, 697–98, 703–704
"Noctes Ambrosianae. No. VI." Mention of Byron's *Vision of Judgment* and *Letter to "Granny Roberts,"* in *The Liberal.*

December, 1822. XII, 769
"Poems, by Bernard Barton." A defence of Byron's poetry.

March, 1823. XIII, 322–23
"Love; a Poem." Wilson (?). Ebenezer Elliot's strictures on Byron are laughed at. Any three consecutive stanzas of *Childe Harold* are "worth all that ever was written by all the Elliots."

April, 1823. XIII, 398–99
"New from Paddy." Byron's *Heaven and Earth* reflects some Cockneyisms.

66 Ferrier, Wilson's *Essays,* I, 401–408 correspond to pp. 175–76, 176–77, and 185–87 of this article.

May, 1823. XIII, 510–11
"French Poets of the Present Day." Lamartine is compared with Byron.

May, 1823. XIII, 563
"The Vicompte de Soligny." Lockhart.[67] Count de Soligny [i.e., Peter George Patmore] likens Byron to a mighty vessel upon the sea.

June, 1823. XIII, 663
"The Cambridge Tart." A poem on Byron's taking a bear to Cambridge is quoted.

June, 1823. XIII, 687
"Criticism." Moore and Byron are "bright stars."

July, 1823. XIV, 87
"On the last Number of the Quarterly Review." Maginn.[68] Southey hits at Byron in *Joan of Arc.*

July, 1823. XIV, 99
"Lord Byron and Mr. Landor." "Idoloclastes" points out that Byron, in a note to *The Island,* criticizes Landor.

October, 1823. XIV, 467
"Mr. Blaquiere's Report on Greece." Lockhart.[69] Byron is in Greece.

December, 1823. XIV, 672
"Beauty." John Bull and Byron agree "cant" is "the prevailing moral feature of the age we live in."

January, 1824. XV, 51
"Hajji Baba of Ispahan." Byron denied writing *Anastatius.*

67 Hildyard, *Lockhart's Literary Criticism,* 155; also Mrs. Gordon, *Christopher North,* 260.

68 Wardle, " 'Timothy Tickler's' Irish Blood," *The Review of English Studies,* XVIII, October, 1942, 487.

69 Hildyard, *Lockhart's Literary Criticism,* 155.

April, 1824. XV, 371
"Noctes Ambrosianae. No. XIV." Byron is a sorry Leander.

April, 1824. XV, 406–407
"Ballantyne's Novelist's Library." Lord Byron's quizzes on his contemporaries are not ill-natured: "Nobody believes that Lord Byron really despises Wordsworth's poetry."

June, 1824. XV, 620–22
"Goethe's Wilhelm Meister." Byron rates Goethe first among his contemporaries. Byron is Goethe's debtor.

November, 1824. XVI, 591–94, 597–98
"Noctes Ambrosianae. No. XVII." Maginn in collaboration.[70] Hogg admits Byron had his faults.

January, 1825. XVII, 69
"Wadd on Corpulency" &c. Facetious mention in passing of Byron's obesity and his dieting.

February, 1825. XVII, 225
"New Sayings and Doings." "Byron could not paint the *roué* without betraying the *roué* in himself."

April, 1825. XVII, 475–76
"MS. Notes on the last Number of the Quarterly Review." Gifford did not particularly value Wordsworth, Scott, or Byron.

May, 1825. XVII, 507–10
"Sir Egerton Brydges's Recollections." Lockhart.[71] Brydges's observations on Byron are refuted.

July, 1825. XVIII, 131
"Plagiarism by Mr. Thomas Campbell." Campbell's "Last Man" is not an imitation of Byron's "Darkness."

70 Wardle, "The Authorship of the *Noctes Ambrosianae*," *Modern Philology*, XLII, August, 1944, 14–15. Hildyard, *Lockhart's Literary Criticism*, 155, assigns to Lockhart, but "doubtful."

71 Hildyard, *ibid.*

October, 1825. XVIII, 400

"Byron." Galt, in the introduction to a letter written by Byron, states that he publishes the letter because it shows Byron's "spirit in a more amiable and kinder character than the invidious part of the world has been willing to allow it."

4. *Incidental Mention of Byron's Name or of his Works*

(An asterisk refers to a contemporary work on Byron included in "Works preparing for Publication" of "Monthly List of New Publications" at the end of each number of *Maga*.)

I, 81, 84, 252, 270, 417, *426; II, "Notices from the Editor" for October, 1817 (Lockhart?), 11 n., 195, 656; III, 83, 405; IV, 62, 212, *365, 406, 563 (Lockhart), 618, *625, 681, 690; V, *107, *243, *357, *492, 548, *614, 629, 699; VI, 202, *221, *345, 645, 675, *716; VII, 303; VIII, 3, 4, 5, 24, 26 (Lockhart),[72] 363, 394, 417, 537, 608, *698; IX, 39–40 (T[homas] D[oubleday]), 75, 85, 191 (D. M. Moir), 198, 264, 277 (D. M. Moir), 281, 284 (T[homas] D[oubleday]), 346 (Wilson?), 466, 507; X, 49, 103, 106, 148, *229, 268, 312, 313, 327, 432, 477, 510, 545, *597; XI, Preface *v,* 183, 280, 285, 329, 332, 346, *372, *375, 478, 508, 588, 649, 686, *756; XII, 66, 71, 85, 161, 167, 187 (Wilson),[73] 198, 226, 236, *241, 433, 434, 471, 479, 531, 590n., 726, 727, 775; XIII, 7, 51, 168, 172, 207, 278, 280, 346, 384, 397, 434, 533 (Lockhart),[72] 580, 605, 661; XIV, 156, 161 (Wilson),[74] 202, 226 (Lockhart and Maginn),[75] 254 (T[homas] D[oubleday]), 310 (Maginn),[75] 318–19, 321 (Lock-

[72] *Ibid.,* 154, 155.

[73] Ferrier, Wilson's *Essays,* I, 401–408, correspond to pp. 175–76, 176–77, and 185–87 of this article.

[74] In this review of Irving's *Orations,* the author refers, on the first page, to his earlier article, "The Gormandizing School of Eloquence"—a piece written by Wilson.—Mrs. Gordon, *Christopher North,* 262. Wilson also reviewed Irving's *Heaven and Hell* in September, 1823.—*Ibid.,* 266.

[75] Wardle, " 'Timothy Tickler's' Irish Blood," *The Review of English Studies,* XVIII, October, 1942, 488.

hart),[76] 342 (Wilson),[77] 346 (Wilson),[77] 488–89, 491–92, 495, 500 (Wilson and Maginn?),[78] 525, 555, 557, 560, *610, 700 (Maginn);[75] XV, 61, 101 (Maginn),[75] 196, 208, 224, 263, 264, 317, 602, 603 (Maginn and another),[79] 638 (Maginn and Lockhart),[79] 703 (Maginn),[75] *727; XVI, 67, *117, 162, 165, 178 (Lockhart),[72] 182 (Maginn),[75] 225 (Maginn),[75] 237, 239–40 (Lockhart),[80] *353, *354, *608, 716 (Maginn),[75] *725; XVII, 71, 223, *234, 461, 487, 623, *628, *631, *752; XVIII, *251, 500 (Wilson),[81] *514.

76 *Ibid.* See also n. 24 in the preceding first section.

77 Mrs. Gordon, *Christopher North,* 266.

78 Wardle, "The Authorship of the *Noctes Ambrosianae,*" *Modern Philology,* XLII, August, 1944, 13.

79 See Wardle, "Who Was Morgan Odoherty?" *PMLA,* LVIII, September, 1943, 726.

80 Same as n. 78, p. 14.

81 Ferrier credits the piece to Wilson in his edition of the *Noctes Ambrosianae.*

APPENDIX B

Faublas as a source of Don Juan

In his *Letter to Byron on Don Juan,* p. 92, Lockhart's remark that the author of *Don Juan* has taken "some warm touches from Peregrine Proteus" is hardly justified. In Christoph Martin Wieland's *Geheime Geschichte des Philosophen Peregrinus Proteus,* Proteus, a youth of eighteen, totally inexperienced in love, is seduced by his cousin Callippe. As she drags him, half-fainting with passion, to her couch, her aged husband Menocrates thunders at the door of the bedchamber—and Proteus jumps out of a window: a tame anticlimax to a skilfully built-up intrigue. Byron had read Wieland in translation,[1] but the situation of Proteus in the German novel and the situation of Don Juan in the first canto of the English poem have only a general similarity that might be paralleled in any number of famous stories. On the other hand, Lockhart's contention is closer to fact when he notes, pp. 91–92, that Byron borrows from Louvet de Couvray's *Faublas* not only "hints," but "sketches" of characters in certain situations. Lockhart remarks of *Faublas* to Byron, "You know it excellently well."

1 ". . . I have read *nothing* of Adolph Mullner's . . . and much less of Goethe, and Schiller, and Wieland, than I could wish. I only know them through the medium of English, French, and Italian translations."—"Extracts from a Diary" (1821), Byron, *Letters and Journals,* V, 171.

The four volumes of *Les Aventures du Chevalier de Faublas,* 1787–89, by Louvet de Couvray, form a satire on the loose social morals under Louis XVI. In these volumes the hero is a youth of sixteen who, as Couvray says in his "Preface,"[2] represents the language and manners of the young people of France. The author characterizes his work as "light and frivolous on the surface, but of deep moral intent." It deals wholly with unfaithful wives, debased libertines, women willing to be seduced, and ill-assorted marriages. It contains many humorous and ludicrous incidents, but becomes decidedly tiresome because of their sameness. Apparently the French work was the *ne plus ultra* of scandalous literature in Lockhart's day. Concerning his own novel *Adam Blair,* Lockhart wrote Christie, March 20, 1822: "Some of the low cattle here are saying, and printing, that it is fit for the same shelf with 'Faublas,' and another book unmentionable."[3] Certainly Byron emphasizes the excesses of youthful passion, but in humor, variety, and dazzling satire *Don Juan* utterly surpasses the French novel.

Lockhart's specific charge in the *Letter to Lord Byron on Don Juan,* p. 92, that Byron's "fine Spanish lady" was taken from Couvray's Marquise de B. is generally true if any definite fine Spanish lady be a necessary original. The Marquise, like Julia, was in her middle twenties, and her lover was a youth of only sixteen and totally inexperienced in love. Caught with her lover in each story, the lady was able to deceive her angry husband, temporarily at least. But Byron, in his rich inventiveness, quickly finishes with Julia: the Marquise through four volumes continues freely to compromise herself and the Chevalier de

2 (Paris, A. Tarvien, 1825, 4 vols.), I, 37–44.

3 Lang, *Life of Lockhart,* I, 302.

Faublas, until her husband catches the pair *flagrante delicto,* attempts to stab Faublas but instead runs his wife through with his sword, and young Faublas goes crazy. Haidee, as Lockhart also claims, p. 92, was in her inexperience and unprotected situation similar to the Countess de Lignolle of Couvray. Also in her passionate first love and entire self-forgetfulness, she is the Countess over again. Since Lockhart's *Letter* appeared in July, 1821, some weeks before Cantos III, IV, and V of *Don Juan* were published, he can here refer only to the first two cantos. If he had known it, he would have been struck by the fact that Haidee and the Countess suffered similar tragic fates, each lady dying with her unborn child. (Cries off stage.)

Maginn or Lockhart in *Blackwood's Magazine* of July, 1823,[4] also claims that Byron owes a debt to Couvray for his seraglio scene. Byron and Couvray both use the stock device of disguise obtained by dressing men in women's clothes to assist their lovers in their intrigues. Couvray, however, employs this stratagem—and also that of dressing women in men's clothes—throughout the whole of his novel. The critic continues by saying that Byron "adopts the filthy tone of Faublas, without, in any one passage, (I mean of these three new cantos,) rivalling the sparkle of Louvet's wit—far less the elegance of Louvet's language."

But the sarcastic implication in *Blackwood's Magazine* of February, 1825,[5] that *Don Juan* is not a mere imitation of *Faublas* is more than justified. *Don Juan* and the French novel (and I don't know how many other works)

4 "Tickler on Don Juan," *Blackwood's Magazine,* XIV, July, 1823, 90. For authorship, see Appendix A.

5 "Lord Byron," *Blackwood's Magazine,* XVII, February, 1825, 132.

have general similarity in certain situations, but Couvray's portrayal of society results in a cardboard "tragedy of manners." Byron's epic satire with its kaleidoscopic variety could use *Faublas* only incidentally.

APPENDIX C

Two Letters: Southey, etc.

Southey's letter to Hogg is in the National Library of Scotland. Here follows a copy of the manuscript original, most of which has been printed in Charles Rogers's The Modern Scottish Minstrel; or the Songs of Scotland of the Past Half Century *[Edinburgh, A. & C. Black, 1855–57, 6 vols.], II, 21–22. Rogers prints also Southey's letter to Hogg of December 1, 1814, and quotes Southey's letter to Grosvenor Bedford, December 22, 1814, on Hogg's opinion of Jeffrey's review of* Roderick *from Cuthbert Southey's edition of his father's letters, IV, 93–94. On April 11, 1851, Lockhart wrote John Wilson: "How good was Hogg's communicating to Southey what Jeffrey said about his being 'about as conceited a fellow as his neighbour Wordsworth.' To be sure they were both magnificent peacocks!"—Lang,* Life of Lockhart, *II, 277.*

Of the communication here printed the first quarter-page (affecting both sides) is missing. The epistle is addressed to "Mr. James Hogg The Ettrick Shepherd Edinburgh.")

I am truly obliged to you for the solicitude which you express concerning the treatment Roderick may experience in the Edinburgh Review, & truly gratified by it, notwithstanding my perfect indifference as to the object in question. But you little know me if you imagine that any thoughts of fear or favour would make me abstain from speaking publicly of Jeffrey as I think he deserves. I despise his commendation & I defy his malice. *He* crush the Excursion!!! Tell him that he might as easily crush Skiddaw. For myself, *popularity* is not the mark I shoot at; if it were I should not write such poems as Roderick; & Jeffrey can no more stand in my way to *fame,* than Tom Thumb could stand in my way in the street.

He knows that he has dealt unfairly & maliciously by me; he knows that the world knows it, that his very friends know it, & that if he attacks Roderick as he did Madoc & Kehama it will universally be imputed to personal ill-will. On the other hand he cannot commend the poem without the most flagrant inconsistency; this would be confessing that he has wronged me in the former instances; for no man will pretend to say that Madoc does not bear marks of the same hand as Roderick;—it has the same character of language, thought & feeling; it is of the same ore & mint; & if the one poem be bad, the other cannot possibly be otherwise. The irritation of the *nettling* (as you term it) which he has already received . . . [*portion of page torn off*] . . . part he may take my conduct towards him will be the same. I consider him a public nuisance & shall deal with him accordingly.

Nettling is a gentle term for what he has to undergo. In due season he shall be *scorpion'd* & *rattlesnaked.* When I take him in hand it shall be to dissect him alive, & make a preparation [?] of him to be exhibited *in terrorem,* an example to all future pretenders to criticism. He has a forehead of native brass,—& I will write upon it with aqua-fortis. I will serve him up to the public like a Turkey's gizzard, sliced, scored, pepperd, salted, kiaun'd, grilled & bedevilled. I will bring him to justice: he shall be executed in prose, & gibbeted in verse, & the Lord have mercy on his soul!

You wish all quartos in hell. Provided the Devil would buy up the edition of Roderick I should have no objection to consign it there. It has however made good speed in the world, & ere long I shall send you the poem in a more commodious shape, for Ballantyne is at this time reprinting it.

I finished my official ode a few days ago. It is without rhyme,

& as unlike other official odes in matter as in form; for its object is to recommend as the two great objects of policy general education, & extensive colonization. At present I am chiefly occupied upon the history of Brazil which is in the press—a work of great labour

The ladies here all desire to be kindly remembered to you. I have ordered the Pilgrims of the Sun & we look for it with expectations that I am sure will not be disappointed. God bless you Yrs very truly

Robert Southey

Keswick 24 Dec. 1814.

(Lockhart's letter to William Maginn was presumably written between May 17 and June, 1824; for though Byron died on April 19, the news of his death did not reach John Murray until May 14, and the Memoirs were burned a few days later; and the fifteenth number of the Noctes Ambrosianae *appears in* Blackwood's Magazine *of June, 1824. Andrew Lang alludes to the letter in his* Life of Lockhart, *I, 133: "In an unpublished note to Maginn, at the time of Byron's death, Lockhart says that 'Blackwood will not have it,' that is, an attack on Byron, proposed by the Irish writer, which Lockhart deprecates himself." The letter mentioned by Lang is in the Pierpont Morgan Library, New York City. Here follows a copy of the manuscript original, most of which appears in Professor Ralph M. Wardle's "Authorship of the* Noctes Ambrosianae," Modern Philology, *XLII, August, 1944, 14.)*

I return w thanks the books you lent me

Dear Doctor

It is a horrid idea of yours to run down Byron dead. It is quite a punch bred notion & you cd not say so impransus.[1] Blackwood, besides, *will* not have it so.

1 *Impransus:* that has not breakfasted, fasting.

My fancy is to have a noble "Noctes" entirely devoted to him. Do you take up Timothy [Tickler] & make him abuse Byron as heartily as heartily [*sic*] as he pleases. Be Odoherty his defender & eulogist mordicus This part I wd fain undertake. I have written to the Professor [John Wilson] to write a flaming speech of North proposing the Memory of the Defunct.[2] I shall also do Hogg. In short do your bits of dialogue introducing any songs—anecdotes—scraps real or imaginary of the Memoirs &c &c of which work Timothy shd have seen a copy These materials I undertake to work up into a fine harmonious whole, cramming into 20 pages as much of truth & of humbug as the Public have recently met with in any similar space. Give us a first rate *Lament* by Odoherty[3]—and I will do ditto for Hogg Be sure you tell all (more than all if you like) that you know or suspect about Moore's concern in the burning business And do all this *instanter* or not at all. . . . . .[*sic:* nothing omitted].

I beg my best respects to the ladies also to Foster & the rest of the Blue Postian heroes

Yours
JGL

2 Since "Christopher North" does not appear in this *Noctes,* Wilson must not have responded.

3 "Odoherty" sings "Lament for Lord Byron" to the air of "The Last Rose of Summer."

INDEX